ANXIOUS ATTACHMENT RECOVERY: THE 8-STEP PLAN

STOP WORRYING, BEAT OVERTHINKING, AND FEEL SECURE IN YOUR RELATIONSHIPS

CHASE HILL

Copyright © 2024 by Chase Hill

All rights reserved.

The content contained within this book may not be reproduced, duplicated or transmitted without direct written permission from the author or the publisher.

Under no circumstances will any blame or legal responsibility be held against the publisher, or author, for any damages, reparation, or monetary loss due to the information contained within this book. Either directly or indirectly.

Legal Notice:

This book is copyright protected. This book is only for personal use. You cannot amend, distribute, sell, use, quote or paraphrase any part, or the content within this book, without the consent of the author or publisher.

Disclaimer Notice:

Please note the information contained within this document is for educational and entertainment purposes only. All effort has been executed to present accurate, up to date, and reliable, complete information. No warranties of any kind are declared or implied. Readers acknowledge that the author is not engaging in the rendering of legal, financial, medical or professional advice. The content within this book has been derived from various sources. Please consult a licensed professional before attempting any techniques outlined in this book.

By reading this document, the reader agrees that under no circumstances is the author responsible for any losses, direct or indirect, which are incurred as a result of the use of information contained within this document, including, but not limited to, — errors, omissions, or inaccuracies.

CONTENTS

A Free Gift to Our Readers	5
Introduction	7
Step One: A Look at Attachment Styles	13
Step Two: The Why Behind the Worry	25
Step Three: From Anxiety to Asset	41
Step Four: Inward Bound	54
Step Five: Soothing the Mind	76
Step Six: Solid Relationships	96
Step Seven: Confidence, Your New Friend	121
Step Eight: Me-Time and We-Time	137
Conclusion	157
Bibliography	175

A FREE GIFT TO OUR READERS

29 WAYS TO OVERCOME NEGATIVE THOUGHTS

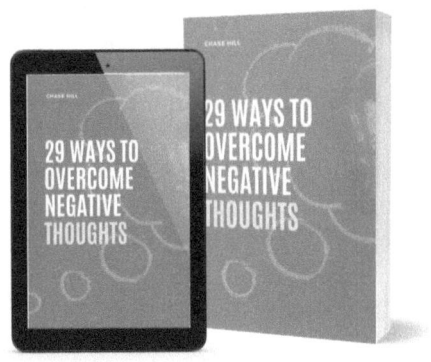

I'd like to give you a gift as a way of saying thanks for your purchase!

In *29 Ways to Overcome Negative Thoughts*, you'll find:

- 10 Strategies to Reduce Negativity in Your Life
- 7 Steps to Quickly Stop Negative Thoughts

- 12 Powerful Tips to Beat Negative Thinking

To receive your Free Ebook, visit the link:

free.chasehillbooks.com

Alternatively, you can scan the QR-code below:

If you have any difficulty downloading the ebook, contact me at **chase@chasehillbooks.com**, and I'll send you a copy as soon as possible.

INTRODUCTION

Shay sits down for a quick coffee and grabs her phone to send her boyfriend a message. Staring at the screen, she sees the two ticks turn blue and waits for the *"typing"* message to appear. When it doesn't, she starts to worry, and after a minute, she is close to full-blown panic. She sends another message, then another, and after 12 messages in a few minutes, her mind is racing. She fears the worst. Not that her boyfriend has had an accident but that he doesn't love her anymore.

The weight on her chest is making it hard for her to breathe, so she calls her boyfriend. He finally picks up, and Shay can tell in his tone that he is frustrated. She now fears they are heading for another one of their arguments. "This is it," she thinks. "This is going to be the time he leaves me." Despite her boyfriend's logical explanation as to why he can't reply to her messages, nothing can calm her anxiety.

Shay's boyfriend has never given her reason to doubt. Her accusations of infidelity when he goes away for a weekend with friends are unjust. The evenings are spent in tears as he tries to reassure her that she is loved little comfort. The only change she has noticed is the increase in arguments as her boyfriend becomes increasingly overwhelmed by her neediness.

It's not the first time that Shay has noticed this. She has seen this happen in her past relationships, even as far back as her late teens. Now, in her early 30s, she knows what is about to happen.

But there is something different about this time. Maybe it's her age. Shay knows she isn't old, but she also knows that if there is any chance of her fulfilling her dream to start a family, something has to change. The answer isn't a new relationship where her fear of abandonment would rear its ugly head again. Shay decides it's time to get help!

From the outside, anxious attachment may seem like it's just a deep fear of being loved and needed, but when you scratch away the surface, it's more complex. This pattern of behavior comes from core needs not being met, even as far back as infancy. The anxiety stems from the fear that others will see you for who you really are, your flaws and all, and deem you unworthy of love.

In an attempt to prevent this from happening, you may have noticed you have fallen into the trap of people pleasing, going out of your way to satisfy the needs of others to the point of exhaustion. On the other end of the scale, you may find yourself self-sabotaging relationships, causing them to end prematurely. After all, if it's going to end, it's better sooner than later. These acts indicate extremely low self-esteem regardless of where you fall on this spectrum.

Afterward, the cycle starts! Low self-esteem sparks negative thought patterns about yourself. You may feel useless in relationships, believe you don't deserve to be happy, and think you are just unlovable. This can then trigger an emotional rollercoaster, causing feelings of insecurity, doubting yourself and your abilities, and, to an extent, the frustration of getting yourself into another situation where you depend on someone instead of being an independent adult.

And after all that, you haven't even addressed the biggest problem. For a relationship like this to work, something has to change naturally. Let's go back to Shay's case. There was nothing more her boyfriend could do to reassure her, and there was nothing else he could do differently. It wouldn't be fair to expect Shay to start demanding changes from her boyfriend. The change needs to come from within. Change is never easy, and like Shay, you are the only person who can be held responsible for making this change.

That doesn't mean to say there isn't guidance and support for you! The strategies and techniques in this book have been shaped by both research and real-world experience to help you build mental resilience, emotional strength, and assertiveness. With these methods, you'll find a practical, manageable structure to overcome the problems you've been battling for years.

Especially evolved for anxious attachment, the Feel-Good framework will unveil how you can conquer relationship anxiety, discover and develop self-awareness, and quiet anxious thoughts.

Every chapter of this book is a small step toward building confident and fulfilling relationships. We'll start by exploring attachment styles to help you identify patterns in your interactions. You will understand what it takes to experience deeper connections while you build confidence and self-esteem. In the end, it's all about finding the perfect balance between independence and togetherness as you look forward to positive outcomes throughout this transformative process.

The result? You will finally be able to enjoy secure, stress-free relationships centered on unconditional self-acceptance and self-love. You will be able to be your true, authentic self and feel reassured that your partner genuinely loves you for who you are.

I can sense the eye roll and the "Nothing will work" mentality. I understand you have tried hard to make changes in your relationship but have not seen the results you had hoped for. This doesn't mean you have failed. You will soon see that breaking free from anxious attachment isn't as simple as opening up more or stopping overthinking. Instead, this requires your mind and your heart to work together rather than against each other, which may have been the case until now.

As with any problem, regardless of whether it stems from the heart or the head, before taking steps to overcome and transform, it's necessary to get to the bottom of attachment theory and how to recognize attachment styles.

STEP ONE: A LOOK AT ATTACHMENT STYLES

I am a part of all that I have met.

ALFRED TENNYSON

What interests me about Tennyson's words is how much of a profound impact the people we meet have on our lives.

It doesn't have to be our family or closest friends who add to who we are as a person today. Even brief acquaintances can change who we are. But what makes us attach to some and not so much to others? Let's begin by understanding what attachment actually is.

DEFINING ATTACHMENT

Back in 1935, Konrad Lorenz experimented with gosling eggs. He took a batch of gosling eggs and divided them into two groups. One group was kept with the natural mother, while the other was hatched in an incubator.

The first living thing the incubator goslings saw was Lorenz, and they began to follow him around. Later, when both groups of goslings were mixed together, both the mother and Lorenz were present. The goslings that had first seen Lorenz separated from the rest, and both groups began to follow him (Study Mind, 2023).

This study not only provides insight into animal behavior but also highlights the significance of attachments, which are essential for humans and begin right from the moment of birth.

An attachment is an emotional bond that connects people regardless of time and space. Attachments can be a source of significant joy, such as falling in love and having children. At the same time, disruptions or breaks in our attachments, like the loss of a loved one, can cause immense distress.

Much of our ability for healthy attachments comes from the very first attachment we experience and the first year of our lives, and more on this topic will be discussed later.

At this point, it's important to recognize that these early attachments play a crucial role in future relationships and are also a survival instinct. Close early attachments, whether human or animal, keep a child close to their caregiver, increasing their chances of survival!

ATTACHMENT THEORY

Attachment theory is the psychological explanation for the bonds between people, not just a child and caregiver, but also within romantic relationships and other long-term forms of relationships.

Previous behavioral theories suggested that our attachments were learned behaviors, meaning that the caregiver provides a child with food (nourishment), and an attachment is formed. However, John Bowlby, a psychoanalyst, believed that problems adults faced in terms of health and behavior could stem from early childhood.

It was actually Lorenz's research into imprinting that influenced Bowlby. He disagreed with the theory that attachment was learned. This was because a child suffering from anxiety separation wasn't calmed by being fed. It was his time as a psychiatrist in London that led him to treat emotionally troubled children, and he focused his attention on their relationships with their mothers, which then led to the development of attachment theory.

Bowlby's theory was that babies displayed built-in mechanisms, such as crying and smiling, as a way of remaining close to their caregiver. This serves for both survival and as a way of seeking safety and support. How the caregiver responds to babies impacts their feelings of security. If a parent responds with warmth and affection, the child will grow up to have a better view of themselves and others and have healthy relationships.

On the other hand, those who were separated from their caregiver, especially the mother, went on to have long-lasting problems. When children's needs aren't met, they struggle to develop a sense of security, which can impede how they explore the world around them.

Throughout his research and observations, Bowlby discovered four characteristics of attachment:

1. Proximity maintenance: The desire to be near those we are attached to.

2. Safe haven: When faced with fear or threats, we return to the people we are attached to for safety and comfort.

3. Secure base: We leave to explore but return to our attached figures.

4. Separation distress: When the attached person isn't around, we are anxious.

Bowlby also hypothesized that it was the first two years of an infant's life when attachment was most critical. During this time, you can see a behavioral system as attachment develops.

The first stage is called pre-attachment and is split into two phases. In the first 8 weeks, babies babble, cry and smile to attract attention from a caregiver. They are able to recognize each caregiver, but their behaviors aren't directed at one in particular.

From 2 to 6 months, their behaviors are now directed at one caregiver. They may start to follow one around more than the other and become clingy to their preferred caregiver. By the end of their first year, babies can display different types of behavior to stay close to their caregiver. This is seen when babies cry and fuss when the caregiver leaves, seek closeness when they are scared and are super happy when that caregiver returns.

Finally, when an infant starts gaining mobility, the safer they feel to begin moving away and exploring the more their caregiver is present. The caregiver provides a sense of security, reassuring the infant. If this source of security isn't around, stronger attachment behaviors are seen. A child who tends to be more fearful or is more susceptible to illness and anxiety may also show stronger attachment behaviors.

If you are a parent, please don't start to panic about your child. We know that today, in an ideal world, one parent would be able to remain with the child in these first crucial years, but it's just not practical. Babies go through a phase of preferring one caregiver, but after around 10 months, they are capable of developing attachments with other adults.

So, there is no need to feel guilty if you leave your child with someone who isn't one of the primary caregivers.

THE FOUR ATTACHMENT STYLES

In the 1970s, psychologist Mary Ainsworth took Bowlby's attachment theory and expanded on this with attachment styles. Her "strange situation" study is still considered groundbreaking, and it's what the four attachment styles in adults are still based on, though Ainsworth coined only three from her research.

Children between the ages of 9 and 18 months participated in a 20-minute play session. During this time, the children experienced different sessions with their mother in a room, with their mother and a stranger, with the stronger only, and alone. There were eight sessions in total, so Ainsworth and her colleague Bell were able to observe how the infants behaved when the mother or stranger entered, left, and reentered the room. These interactions were further broken down into two or three minutes each. If the child was comfortable, the time was extended, but at any sign of distress, the sessions were shortened.

The stages were as follows:

- **Stage 1:** mother, infant, and observer enter the room
- **Stage 2:** mother and infant are in the room
- **Stage 3:** stranger enters the room
- **Stage 4:** mother leaves the room
- **Stage 5:** mother reenters, stranger leaves

- **Stage 6:** mother leaves, infant is alone

- **Stage 7:** stranger returns

- **Stage 8:** mother returns, stranger leaves

From Ainsworth and her colleagues' observations, three attachment styles were recognized: secure, resistant, and avoidant.

Secure infants were distressed when their mom left but happy when she returned. They used their mom as a safe base to explore the room and avoided the stranger when she wasn't around. When their mom was present, the infant was friendly toward the stranger.

Resistant infants showed great distress when their mom left, but when she returned, they resisted contact, and some even pushed her away. These infants cried more, explored less, and were fearful of the stranger.

Avoidant infants showed no distress when their mom left and little interest when she returned. They played normally when the stranger was present, and both their mom and stranger were able to comfort these infants equally well (Mcleod, 2024).

In the 1980s, researchers Main and Solomon proposed a fourth attachment style, disorganized-insecure attachment. This occurs when caregivers are inconsistent or unpredictable when parenting and children are easily confused. Children with disorganized-insecure attachment struggle to feel secure with others despite wanting intimacy.

Let's move on to what these attachment styles manifest in adulthood.

Secure Attachment

People with a secure attachment have grown up with secure caregivers. They are able to find reassurance and comfort and feel understood. Caregivers were emotionally available, which led to adults having positive and trusting relationships. Other signs include:

- High self-esteem
- The ability to self-reflect
- Emotional regulation and emotionally available
- Good communication skills
- Able to manage conflicts
- Comfortable being in a relationship and being alone
- Ease in connecting with others

Avoidant Attachment

Parents may have been incredibly strict, but it's more likely they were emotionally and/or physically unavailable. This can cause adults to struggle with any form of intimacy. Adults are often overly independent due to unmet needs during childhood.

They may also:

- Be uncomfortable expressing feelings
- Come across as giving others the cold shoulder
- Have difficulty trusting others
- Prefer spending time alone
- Strongly believe that they don't need people in their lives
- Feel threatened by those who attempt to get close to them

Disorganized Attachment

Sadly, this may stem from abusive parents, who shower children with love only to end up being abusive again. This cycle leaves children very confused and fearful.

This confusion is reflected in adult relationships and can make it difficult to predict their behavior. Disorganized attachment can cause:

- A fear of rejection
- Emotional dysregulation (not being able to regulate emotions)
- Chronic stress and anxiety
- Signs of avoidant and anxious attachment
- Increased risk of mood and personality disorders
- Increased risk of self-harm and substance abuse

Anxious Attachment

This is similar to disorganized attachment but to a lesser degree, where abuse may not have been present. Instead, parents may have switched between coddling and being indifferent, having moments of attentiveness followed by pushing children away. Some common signs of this attachment style are:

• Clinging and difficulties being alone

• Low self-esteem and self-worth

• Intense fear of rejection and abandonment

• Jealousy

• Seeking approval from others

• Sensitive to criticism

• Struggles with trust

It's important to note that attachment styles aren't cut and dry. You probably won't identify with just the traits of anxious anxiety. These styles can also change over time and aren't fixed in stone. Naturally, we are going to take a closer look at anxious attachment in the next chapter, but for now, rather than focusing too much on this particular style, it's a good idea to take some time to reflect back on your childhood in general.

This is also an ideal time to start using a new journal. Journaling has been proven to reduce stress and anxiety, boost emotional regulation, and improve communication. As there will be more moments for self-reflection throughout the book, it makes sense to have all your thoughts and feelings in one place. If you aren't a pen-and-paper person, you could also start a new document on your computer or phone.

For peace of mind, I would recommend password-protecting this, not to stop others from reading it, but to give you the assurance to express yourself openly and honestly without worrying about anyone else judging you.

Here is **step one of the Feel-Good** framework. Don't worry if some of the answers to these questions don't make you feel all that good. Look at this as the antiseptic sting before a wound starts to heal!

- Who were the significant people in your life as you were growing up?

- What was it like for you growing up?

- What positive memories do you have?

- What negative memories do you have?

- What was your relationship like with your parents when you were a young child?

- Did you witness or experience a lot of conflicts?

- Were you often punished as a child, and if so, how?

- Did you feel safe in your home and comforted by your parents?

- If you didn't grow up with your parents, who raised you?

- Have you ever felt threatened by those who raised you?

- Have you ever been rejected by those who raised you?

- Have you lost anyone significant in your life, whether through separation or death?

- How did this loss affect you and impact your life?

- How would you raise your children differently from how you were raised?

These questions will probably point toward an anxious attachment, but there is more to understand about this style in order to begin unraveling its impact on your life and seeing the positive changes you need!

STEP TWO: THE WHY BEHIND THE WORRY

The past influences everything and dictates nothing.

ADAM PHILLIPS

While the first chapter covered attachment theory and the different styles, we need to take a much deeper look into anxious attachment and explore the reasons why you have reached the place where you are in your life today. Naturally, this requires examining your past experiences. Due to the significance of your first attachments, it's normal to explore how you were raised.

It's possible that your parents were abusive, and I am truly sorry if that's the case. It's also possible that your parents weren't perfect, but they were doing the best they could. I know from my own experiences that there was a lack of the same awareness surrounding mental health and child development back in the day, and there certainly weren't as many books for our parents to access and get help and support. This is where the words of Adam Phillips are so important to remember. The past may have gotten you to where you are today, but it doesn't mean it has to hold the same power over your future.

As you work through this chapter, the idea isn't to blame your parents for your anxious attachments because that is only going to cause you more pain. Take Michelle, for example. Michelle's dad was in the military and wasn't around for most of her first year. By the time she was around 10 years old, Michelle noticed that he wasn't all that present when he was at home. His affair led to divorce, and after a messy few years, Michelle stopped speaking to her dad.

As an adult, Michelle struggled to connect with her partners, not because she clung to them because she missed a strong father figure but because she was far too independent. Michelle believed that not needing anyone was a good thing. However, when she took the time to see how this was impacting her mental health, she began to understand that her almost obsessive need to be independent stemmed from her fear of letting someone in, relying on them, and then being abandoned.

Nothing was about to change her past experiences, but only she could determine how her future would plan out. Understanding what her dad did was a painful yet crucial step to learning more about herself. But holding on to the past would only prevent her from moving forward. I strongly encourage you to take the same attitude as we move forward.

ZOOMING IN: WHAT IS ANXIOUS ATTACHMENT?

Before zooming in, let's do a quick recap. Anxious attachment is rooted in the fear of abandonment and rejection. It can cause a severe lack of trust, clinginess, and low self-esteem and confidence. It's also known as preoccupied attachment disorder, where people are nervous about being separated from their partner.

While each person and relationship is going to be different, some common triggers can initiate this fear of abandonment or rejection. One of these triggers that will ring true for many is conflict. The moment you and your partner have an argument, the first place your mind races to is the possibility that it's the end of the relationship. This can even happen during healthy conflict and in new relationships. For someone with an anxious attachment, nothing is more terrifying than the first argument with a new partner.

This is similar to levels of responsiveness. Early on in a relationship, communication is buzzing with messages and maybe calls throughout the day. Once the initial honeymoon phase passes, couples get into a routine of daily communication, which is normally less frequent than those early days. For you, it doesn't matter if you are in your first month or your tenth year, when your partner doesn't reply, you often think the worst. If we are being brutally honest, the worst-case scenario might not be that something bad happened to them but rather that they are no longer interested in a relationship with you!

Every relationship will have its ups and downs, and during difficult times, a partner may express these concerns. When your partner expresses these concerns, you hear the words but aren't listening. Instead, your mind is catastrophizing the information as if it were the end, but your partner never said that. In extreme cases, you may have found yourself sabotaging relationships.

Unfortunately, your actions, intentional or not, tend to push your partner away and create distance between you. Needless to say, this distance is enough to cause you to fear the end even more. Your partner may go out with friends or be stuck at work, just like you, and it's a reason not to spend time with you.

There will also be occasions when partners look for more independence, especially as a relationship progresses. Typically, at the start of a relationship, individuals do everything together. Whether independence comes after the honeymoon period or as a result of increased conflicts, your needs aren't being validated.

Finally, a significant trigger can also be unpredictability, which is often linked to the care someone receives as a child. If a parent were there for you one minute and not the next, there would be increased insecurity when partners aren't consistent with their behavior.

These triggers tend to be more focused on romantic relationships but can also be observed in other types of relationships. Another sign of anxious attachment is people pleasing, which can appear in relationships with partners, parents, friends, and colleagues. In an attempt to not be abandoned or rejected, you will go out of your way to make sure others are happy.

If you happen to be trapped in a toxic relationship, the other person will use this to their advantage. More often than not, you are going out of your way to fulfill the needs of others when they are happy with a lot less.

For example, if you want to feel accepted in the workplace and overcome the fear of losing your job, you might end up taking on more responsibilities than you should and even more than you get paid for.

Your boss and your colleagues would have been happy with you fulfilling your role and not going to the extent of working yourself into the ground.

Let's conclude with a few more signs that might indicate you are stuck in an anxious attachment style:

- You frequently check social media to get more information about someone
- You tend to feel suspicious when things are calm

- You do things that others want, even when you don't want to, and you are aware these actions will cause you more harm than good

- You often ask your partner if they find you attractive

- You avoid ending a relationship even when it's an unhealthy one

- You constantly ask your partner what they think or feel

- You have a negative view of yourself

- You can't solve problems without your partner

- You spend a lot of time ruminating over worst-case scenarios and not just in romantic relationships

Rather than reaching for your phone to check for a like, a share, or a message, let's keep moving forward as we consider how anxiety attachment develops.

LINKING PAST TO PRESENT

As we saw in the first chapter, anxious attachment often stems from our early childhood. This can be because of being apart from caregivers or from caregivers being inconsistent with their parenting, such as being emotionally available and then withdrawing any attention. In these situations, children don't know what to expect and are never sure whether their needs will be met. This also applies to trauma and neglect. The chaotic environment these children grow up in can cause them to become hypervigilant and extremely sensitive to any signs of rejection or abandonment.

Unfortunately, an anxious attachment may even go further back than this. Children who witness a parent's symptoms of anxious attachment are more likely to grow up and develop the same style of attachment. If a parent has grown up in an unpredictable environment, they consider it normal. Unless they have taken steps to overcome their own attachment style, which is unlikely due to the lack of mental health awareness in the past, these "normal behaviors" will stick with them when raising their own children.

In Step One, it seems like moms have received a fair amount of judgment for their potential role, which is a generational issue. In the past, it was much more common for moms to stay at home and dads to be the sole breadwinner. As family dynamics change and fathers become more involved in children's lives, recent research has shown that a father's attachment style can impact a child's level of anxiety all the way into adolescence (Jagoo, 2022). Angry fathers can lead to an anxious father-child attachment. So, it's not just maternal figures who can contribute to anxious attachment.

Relationships a child witnesses can also greatly impact a future relationship style. Parents who argue a lot are more likely to create an unstable environment, especially in terms of emotional stability. Children may feel startled, neglected in times of conflict, or be on the receiving end of parents' anger or frustration. Parents who have either an anxious or avoidant attachment style are harder to co-parent with, leading to more conflict. The result of this can negatively impact a child's social skills, emotional well-being, and coping skills (Busacker, 2022).

It's not just parenting that can cause this type of attachment style. There is some evidence to show that people with anxious attachment have different brain activity, especially in parts of the brain that handle the threat response. Sensorimotor processing is how the brain handles information received by the senses and then integrates it into a particular motor response within the central nervous system. Take, for example, the way your stomach might churn with certain smells, or you pull your hand away when you touch something hot.

To understand how brains may work differently, you also need to understand your peripersonal space, which is the space around your body that you can reach. Another crucial aspect to consider is the parietofrontal cortical network, the part of the sensorimotor processes that respond to things that approach your peripersonal space.

Let's take a look at how the three work together before digging into the research. Imagine you hear a Doberman barking on the other side of the road. Your ears pick up the sound and send a message to your sensorimotor system. As the threat is still on the other side of the road, your central nervous system increases your heart rate. When that dog crosses the road and enters your peripersonal space, close enough to bite you, the parietofrontal cortical network kicks in, and your hand may reach out to protect your body or smack the dog!

The Harvard University Center for Brain Science recruited a group of adults to better understand the workings of the brain and different attachment styles. People with all four attachment styles were present. While functional magnetic resonance images (fMRI) were taken of the brain, the participants were shown images of a human face approaching them and then moving away from them. They were also shown a car approaching and moving away. For those with anxious attachment, there was more activity in the parietofrontal cortical network than in those with other attachment styles (Nasiriavanaki et al., 2021).

What was even more interesting is that this only happened with the image of the human face, and not the car, and only when the face approached. Furthermore, there were no other symptoms associated with their anxious attachment style. Apart from early childhood experiences, your anxious attachment may be due to an over-responsive sensorimotor network!

Research is mixed on whether or not culture has an impact on anxious attachment. Some believe there is no correlation, while others think the correlation is minor. It makes sense that cultures with close family ties and dependence on others may see a greater prevalence of anxious attachment. Society may also play a role depending on its messages regarding relationships. If there is pressure to be in or maintain relationships, someone with an anxious attachment may feel even more anxious with this pressure and fear of abandonment.

THE CYCLE OF WORRY AND INSECURITY

It's not enough that your anxious attachment causes moments of immense doubt and insecurity. It also initiates a chain of responses that fuel your anxiety and fears.

The cycle begins with a trigger or a perceived threat, which then leads to thoughts. Typically, these thoughts end up being catastrophic thinking, where your mind goes straight to the worst-case scenario, or you start to exaggerate the importance of the relationship. That's not to say that your relationship isn't important, but you may think that it is an essential part of who you are and even a central part of your self-worth. Relationships are part of your life, but you should still have a healthy sense of who you are.

Next comes the emotional response, mainly fear and anxiety, which can also trigger strong physical responses. And, in an attempt to find reassurance, your behavior changes, needing validation or evidence that the relationship isn't ending. Your partner may respond, but the relief from anxiety is brief. If you are used to an inconsistent pattern of attention and affection, your mind will be waiting for the next trigger. Here is an example of the cycle:

- **Trigger:** Your partner has to work on Saturday morning.

- **Thought:** They can't be at work, so they must be having an affair; the relationship is over.

- **Emotional response:** You feel sadness and fear about being alone in the future.

- **Behavior:** You're hypervigilant and constantly checking your partner's phone.

- **Outcome:** When no messages are found, you feel relieved.

- **Reinforcement of anxiety:** Your partner arrives home late from work, and the cycle begins again.

This cycle shows that it's not about what a partner does or doesn't do. The only way to break this cycle is to address the underlying securities of your anxious attachment.

THE IMPACT OF ANXIOUS ATTACHMENT

At this point, we don't need to overly rehash the impact of an anxious attachment on relationships. It's like constantly walking on eggshells, and you aren't getting the same relationship satisfaction you should be getting. Instead of joy, you are worried and obsessed about the small details.

This isn't just exhausting for you. Your partner is working overtime to try and fulfill your needs and insecurities, and it's also draining for them, too.

Although most of the attention is on romantic relationships, anxious attachments can affect any type of relationship. You may need a lot of validation from your friends. This can be especially hard in group dynamics, where you fear being left out or replaced. It's common to have problems with a partner and need a friend to talk to for emotional support. However, an anxious attachment can take this to the extreme, and friends may feel overwhelmed by this neediness. This could be caused by a lack of boundaries, which can also cause problems with family members.

Just because you have an anxious attachment, it doesn't necessarily mean that your sibling does too, considering the range of causes. They may have grown up with a secure attachment, and this makes it hard for them to understand why you constantly compete for your parents' attention, affection, and approval.

If you gain this attention, your siblings may feel jealous, sparking conflict between you. Even if you don't get the extra attention, your siblings are likely to feel frustrated.

As for the workplace, you may also notice that you are constantly seeking validation or going out of your way to keep others happy, especially in high-conflict situations. It's possible that working independently is more challenging and that you rely on superiors, which could influence how they perceive your capabilities.

Feedback is a particular struggle, even constructive criticism! When a superior offers feedback, you may focus only on the negative, filtering out any positive information you have been given.

While only listening to the negative, you are adding to a fear of rejection. It's not only that your work isn't good enough, but it's also a feeling that you aren't good enough.

The consequence of this is that you try harder to feel accepted, which puts you at risk of chronic workplace stress and burnout.

Anxious attachment can also increase the risk of histrionic and borderline disorders (Mikulincer & Shaver, 2012). Histrionic personality disorder is a pattern of attention-seeking behaviors and emotional instability. Individuals with this disorder often act dramatically and inappropriately in order to get this attention, but they may also use their appearance and sexuality.

A borderline personality disorder affects the way a person sees themself. In relationships, this can cause instability, impulsiveness, and moments of intensity. Fear of abandonment often triggers strong emotional responses.

Not everyone with an anxious attachment will develop histrionic or borderline disorders. If you are concerned, you may need professional help to manage the symptoms of these disorders, but before that, developing self-awareness is crucial.

THE IMPORTANCE OF SELF-AWARENESS

Have you noticed how much of life is robotic, like you are on a conveyor belt just going through the motions?

When this happens, it's hard to stop and think about our actions, behaviors, thoughts, and emotions. A lack of self-awareness can cause us to ignore thoughts and feelings, which may increase anxiety, depression, and negative behaviors.

On the other hand, self-awareness enables us to calm the constant noise in our minds, take control of our lives, change beliefs, and improve physical and mental well-being.

It allows you to see your positive and not-so-positive habits as well as strengths and areas for improvement. This can be difficult and lead to fear because no one enjoys exploring their flaws.

In Step Four, we will investigate the power of self-awareness in more detail, but for now, this is a good opportunity to take some time to become more aware of your current relationships.

Grab your journal and work through these questions.

- Can you be your true self around your partner?
- Does your partner understand you?

- Do you and your partner share the same sense of humor?

- How important is it that you have the same interests?

- Can you put your hand on your heart and say you trust your partner?

- Can you be honest with your partner?

- Do you feel supported by your partner?

- Do you both share core values?

- On a scale of 1 to 10 (10 being completely), how happy are you in your relationship?

- How have you changed since you have been with your partner?

- How do you handle arguments in your relationship?

- Do you support each other's dreams and goals?

- Do you feel you have a safe space for communication?

- What are some challenges of being in a relationship with you?

- What are your best traits in this relationship?

- How do you show love and affection?

- Are you open to love and affection?

Let's be honest, after understanding the true impact of anxious attachment and reflecting on your relationship, things might be looking a little bleak! It might surprise you to discover that there is actually a positive side to your anxious attachment.

In the next chapter, we are going to see the flip side of negativity and how you can use your attachment as a strength as you work to free yourself from fears and anxiety.

STEP THREE: FROM ANXIETY TO ASSET

Our wounds are often the openings into the best and most beautiful part of us.

DAVID RICHO

It's hard to imagine anything good coming out of something that has caused you so many challenges. But what if you could stop fighting your anxious attachment and put that energy to better use? The first step is recognizing that the wounds caused by your attachment style have certain advantages if you know where to look.

ANOTHER PERSPECTIVE

Your partner leaves for a weekend business trip, and anxiety kicks in. You can't possibly cope for a whole weekend alone, and their excitement only confirms that the relationship is doomed. What positive aspects can be found behind this fear and anxiety? To answer this question, we need to take on another perspective. As you read through this section, I want you to imagine a friend of yours who shares your anxious attachment. It's always easier to show more compassion to others than ourselves!

There is no doubt that those with anxious attachments are completely committed to relationships and aren't scared of intimacy. They easily fall in love, which isn't always a red flag! It means that you are aware of your emotions and are emotionally available. It's also a sign that you know what you want in a relationship and know exactly what that looks like. For example, if you value humor over intelligence and find someone who constantly makes you laugh, it's only natural for oxytocin and dopamine to kick in, whether it's been a few weeks or a few months.

Although there are problems in anxious attachment relationships, which are fueled by a fear of abandonment, the high level of commitment means people are less likely to give up on a relationship when there is trouble. They may not know how to handle the problems, but they don't just throw the towel in like other people may.

Picture your friend being hypervigilant. They pick up on every tiny detail that many others would miss. What if this hypervigilance was seen as a superpower, especially combined with greater emotional awareness? They are highly tuned in to their partner's emotions and needs, and with so much love to give, they are happy to support those needs and feelings. When their partner says they are fine, they can read between the lines and understand that they aren't fine.

Having anxious attachment stems from low self-esteem, but it only refers to how a person views themselves. They likely see their partner in an extremely positive light. When their partner is feeling low, the anxious attacher is there to point out their qualities and help them see themselves more favorably.

The anxious attacher can also be an amazing friend for many of the same reasons as above. They are good at spotting their friends' needs and offering support, working hard to maintain relationships. This can be particularly beneficial for long-distance friendships when contact has a habit of fading.

This worry for friends can often mean that an anxious attachment leads to being the caretaker in the group, with friends feeling safe and comfortable talking about their problems. Again, being a people pleaser is often associated with negative, but as long as friends don't take advantage, it's reassuring knowing a good friend has always got your back and will be there for them if they need it.

Even the workplace can benefit from a person with an anxious attachment. Research carried out by Ein-Dor and Shaver in 2011 led to the Social Defense Theory, which states each attachment style has a benefit and a disadvantage. They proposed that people with anxious attachments were more likely to remember information related to threats, which meant they were more likely to spot a potential threat and warn others (Psychology in Action, n.d.). This hypervigilance is beneficial, as they are better at identifying workplace problems. In fact, this heightened awareness of threats acts as a survival mechanism with friends and partners, too.

The need to be accepted by your friend can be exhausting, but it also means they are hard workers, loyal, and dependable. They stick to the rules so as not to rock the boat. Naturally, other attributes such as commitment, thoughtfulness, and supportiveness can also be advantageous in the workplace.

It's only normal that you have focused on the negative side of your attachment style, and even now, you may not be completely convinced. There are two more benefits to your attachment style that warrant a closer look.

EMPATHY AS A GATEWAY TO DEEPER CONNECTIONS

One of the superpowers we looked at in the previous section was the ability to tune into other people's emotions and needs, which is essentially empathy. Empathy is different from sympathy. Sympathy is about feeling sorry for someone going through a hard time, whereas empathy is the ability to feel the same emotions they are experiencing.

There are three types of empathy in any kind of relationship: cognitive, emotional, and compassionate. Cognitive empathy lets you understand how a person feels and what they might think. Emotional empathy relates to the emotional connection between two people and their feelings about what they are going through. Compassionate empathy allows you to take action based on understanding exactly what that person is going through.

You might struggle with communicating how you feel, but if you are empathetic, you are halfway there. The ability to truly see and feel what someone is going through opens the door to healthy communication, especially when dealing with conflicts.

Imagine a typical argument with your partner over clinginess. Without empathy, you can only see your side of the argument and are stuck in a trap of your fears. With empathy, you can see that your partner genuinely loves you and is concerned about you. But they also need some room to breathe once in a while. Empathy allows you to experience life through their eyes and close gaps in any bridges.

Empathy allows you to practice compassion. When your partner walks through the door, you may have an uncontrollable need to tell them all about your day. However, the empathetic side of you sees that they have had a tough day and need a chance to disconnect before you unload, or maybe they need someone to listen to their concerns. When you don't give this space, and they come across as snappy, empathy will help you understand their behavior.

There is a little bit of a harsh lesson for us in this. Taking a moment to see things from someone else's point of view can help you highlight your flaws or at least areas that you could work on to strengthen your relationships. For example, not rushing for your partner's validation when they walk in the door can show the need for more patience on your behalf, which adds to your self-awareness.

Empathy isn't just about connecting with the perceived negative emotions and potential problems. It's also about feeling their perceived positive emotions, and this can surprisingly be even more beneficial. One study showed that empathizing with positive emotions was five times more beneficial for relationship satisfaction than just empathizing with negative ones (Andreychik, 2017).

Along with these positive effects on your relationships, empathy may also reduce your stress levels. Walking around daily without knowing how other people truly feel can contribute to your stress levels and insecurities, as you constantly question what another person is thinking. You don't need to add to your stress by trying to fix their problems because unless they have specifically asked for your opinion, it's not your responsibility. However, knowing that you understand them can take away their tension and yours.

If you feel your empathy skills could be improved, don't worry. In Step Six, you will be able to work on your empathy and communication skills!

FROM VULNERABILITY TO EMPOWERMENT

In a society where strength and independence are favored, showing any sign of vulnerability is considered a weakness. It's like you are displaying your flaws for everyone to see, and eventually, someone is going to take advantage of them. This is a great misconception.

Brené Brown, a leading expert on empathy and vulnerability, defines vulnerability as "uncertainty, risk, and emotional exposure." She also believes that it's the center of meaningful human experiences. So, how is it that showing your vulnerability can actually be your greatest strength?

Based on Brown's definition, vulnerability is about showing your true emotions, even when you are uncertain or sense a risk. Essentially, the only way you are going to achieve a strong and meaningful relationship is if you open up to the extent where people can see your authentic self, both the good and the bad.

When you try to hide your flaws or weaknesses, people only see the positive qualities and place you on a pedestal. They may keep their distance, physically or emotionally, out of fear of not being good enough. As soon as another person can see that you are a mere, imperfect human like the rest of us, it becomes easier to establish a connection.

That being said, when you consider your past, it's only normal that you have created this emotional wall around you as a form of self-protection. Each time you have been hurt, intentionally or not, another brick has been added to the wall.

This reminds me of a great clip from *The Cleaner* in an episode called "When Marriage Leads to Murder." The wife, played by Helena Bonham Carter, explains how one act can be like a paper cut. It hurts, and you bleed. But the pain of your past is like one papercut after another. It makes sense that you have done what you had to do to protect yourself from that.

Vulnerability doesn't just manifest emotionally. You may also notice physical feelings that add to distress. It's those moments when your heart starts to race when you step out of your comfort zone, the shaking hands when you want to explain something to someone, or the discomfort in your stomach when you feel you are about to get hurt. All of this makes us fear being vulnerable.

Shying away from vulnerability can prevent you from experiencing the immensity of your emotions. Joy is essential for providing us with pleasure, happiness, and positivity.

When fear of vulnerability is blocking your path, you can't

fully embrace joy because there will always be a part of you waiting for the next bad thing to happen.

On the other hand, though shame can be incredibly distressing, its purpose is to show us where we have gone wrong, and without it, there is little room for personal growth.

Research has shown that vulnerability leads to better mental health, greater resilience in times of adversity, and even more bravery (Kumar, 2023). This makes sense. Think back to any time you have found your courage and achieved something you wouldn't have thought possible.

Wasn't there a risk involved? Didn't you have to step out of your comfort zone and be willing to do things that exposed your weaknesses? When you look at things from this perspective, you can see how vulnerability can be a huge asset.

The first step to becoming more vulnerable is to recognize your vulnerabilities and accept them as part of the human experience. And you need to be able to be compassionate toward this whole person. Just because you have flaws doesn't mean they can't be worked on and improved.

Keep this in mind as you answer the following questions:

- What emotion do you feel most often?
- What's the worst thing you have done to someone?

- What do you dislike about yourself?
- What's your biggest insecurity?
- How can you be a better person?
- In what ways do you think other people look down on you?
- How do you define your self-worth?
- What is a quality you have that you are ashamed of?

Next, you need to be able to trust the person you want to be vulnerable with. For this, you have to remember that your partner, or any other person you want to be close to, is not the same person as those who have hurt you in the past. The people in your life now deserve to be treated as the individuals they are. While there are people out there with malicious intentions, there are also plenty who are worth trusting.

It's important that you take small steps toward vulnerability. It's one thing to step out of your comfort zone, and it's another to leap out of it so far that you cause yourself unnecessary suffering. Begin by sharing a personal detail that you would normally keep private with someone close to you or talking about mistakes you have made. The next time you feel fear, guilt, or shame, sit with it and accept it instead of hiding from it or burying it. If you keep taking these small steps each day, you will notice the walls around you coming down!

FEELING GOOD AGAIN

You have come a long way in a short time. Understanding the true depths of your anxious attachment and its roots. While there are benefits to this attachment style, it's still not one that you want to hold onto.

Developing a secure attachment will enable you to maintain the positives but also overcome everything that's holding back your relationships.

To do this, we are going to go back to the **Feel-Good** framework and work on the following areas of life:

- Tackling relationship anxieties

- Discovering and developing self-awareness

- Quietening anxious thoughts

- Deepening connections

- Building confidence and self-esteem

- Balancing independence and togetherness

The benefits of this transformative process are twofold. First, you will see massive advancements in your relationships. Your hypervigilance and anxiety will be calmed and replaced with strong bonds and trust.

Rather than expecting the worst, you will start to see the good intentions of others, especially when you begin to boost your levels of empathy.

However, you shouldn't just embark on this change for others. It will bring about so many positives for you as an individual. As you lower your levels of distress and take steps to better mental health with better emotional regulation skills, you will change the way you view yourself, gaining confidence, self-esteem, and a healthy sense of self-worth.

I know you still have this unsettling need to please your partner and others around you, but remember that you aren't just going to take these steps for them.

On that final note, take some time to think about what you want to achieve for yourself by answering the following questions:

• What habit do you have that you want to stop as soon as possible?

• What skill do you want to learn in the next month?

• What's the biggest behavioral change you hope to achieve in the next 2 months?

• Where do you see yourself in 6 months from now?

• What can you do in the upcoming year that would make you feel proud of yourself?

The detailed answers to these questions will be the guide to your path to personal growth, and along with this growth will come the freedom from your anxious attachment style.

It's time to lay the foundations for this exciting change by going back to self-awareness and seeking a better understanding of yourself and your relationships!

STEP FOUR: INWARD BOUND

Knowing yourself is the beginning of all wisdom.

ARISTOTLE

Do you think you really know yourself? It's a profound question! You may know a decent amount about who you are, your likes and dislikes, what makes you tick, and what is important to you, but these can all be considered the surface layer of you.

Knowing your true self is about understanding your strengths, dreams and desires, past experiences that shape the story you tell yourself, and your perspectives, beliefs, and values. We consider many of these aspects in fleeting moments instead of incorporating them into our lives.

Some people feel that their true self changes slightly over

time, but others have a more fluid approach and that new experiences can shift your self-identity.

For those with an anxious attachment, your sense of who you are may well be all over the place, especially if you have changed any aspect that adds to your self-identity to please others. Needless to say, children who grow up with a secure attachment have a strong sense of identity.

In order to develop an understanding of your authentic self, it's necessary to go inward-bound!

THE POWER OF SELF-AWARENESS

Let's begin with a quick recap. Self-awareness is the ability to pay attention to yourself, your thoughts, emotions, and actions and then ensure that all of these align with your personal standards and beliefs. It enables you to manage emotions and make sure others understand you correctly.

Self-awareness can be seen as two different types. Public self-awareness refers to being aware of how we appear to others. It's what encourages us to stick to society's norms and behave in acceptable ways.

You may have noticed that your constant concern about what people think of you has taken this consciousness into self-consciousness.

This excessive amount of awareness and worry in public can lead to those changes that deviate from your authenticity.

Private self-awareness is the practice of introspectiveness in order to comprehend your own physical and emotional internal state. It's about noticing the physical symptoms behind your emotions that you might be aware of, but others aren't.

These two types of self-awareness combined allow for a clear and objective view of yourself. Both are also part of self-awareness theory, the idea that you are a separate entity from your thoughts.

By understanding this difference, self-aware people can look at their current behavior and see how it differs from their internal standards, values, and beliefs, contributing to greater self-control.

Being self-aware is the cornerstone of empathy. When you are in touch with your feelings and can communicate them, you encourage others to do the same, and when a person opens up about their feelings, you are no longer making assumptions that could lead to miscommunications.

It's like shining a bright light that provides clarity within relationships. Together, you can make better decisions with less chance of conflict.

This has amazing benefits for your future and your future relationship. Self-awareness is also contagious. The more others see you doing it, the more they will too. Aside from further deepening your relationship, this is an essential life skill to teach your children if you have them.

You may wonder how self-awareness can lead to better decision-making skills. Think about a time that you reacted based on your emotions before having all the information.

For example, you are agreeing to do something your friends want to do because you want to avoid causing problems with the plans. But then, it turns out the plans are even more dreadful than you had imagined.

If you had taken a step back from your initial emotion and considered all the facts and whether they aligned with your standards, you would have made a more informed decision.

As we concluded in the last chapter, your journey isn't just about your relationships. Self-awareness can do wonders for your own well-being. It gives you opportunities to see when patterns in behavior add to poor mental health. If you are struggling with anxiety or depression, recognizing the symptoms can help you better manage them instead of them getting out of control.

It's also possible that self-awareness can positively impact your physical health. When you are in tune with your physical responses, it's easier to spot when something isn't right and uncover potential health risks earlier on. With better decision-making skills, you are also more inclined to make healthy lifestyle choices.

Finally, if you have ever thought that your partner completes you, you will soon discover how practicing self-awareness will allow you to feel like a whole, independent person. This goes back to your journey to personal growth for yourself and your relationships.

11 PRACTICAL STEPS TO BUILD SELF-AWARENESS

There is a little bit of irony when it comes to self-awareness. When Dr. Tasha Eurich, an organizational psychologist, and her team carried out research, they discovered that 95 percent of people thought themselves to be self-aware. However, only 10 to 15 percent of the participants matched the criteria for self-awareness (The Forem, 2023). The lesson here is that you may think you are doing well in self-awareness, but the following 12 steps may help you to see otherwise.

Check in with your awareness wheel

While the awareness wheel has several versions, Dr. Dan Siegel's is evidence-based and used as a visual metaphor to link consciousness with the focus of attention (Dr. Dan Siegel, n.d.). The core understandings of awareness are in the center of the wheel: clear, aware, receptive, open, peaceful, and calm.

To achieve this, we can focus on the outer elements of the wheel. These include the first five senses (touch, taste, smell, sight, and hearing), the sixth sense of the interior body, the seventh of mental activities, and the eighth of interconnectedness. Essentially, the wheel helps you understand that true awareness goes beyond the first five senses.

Know your strengths and weaknesses

To objectively understand your strengths and weaknesses, it's wise to carry out a SWOT analysis. SWOT stands for Strengths, Weaknesses, Opportunities, and Threats.

The SWOT analysis is typically used for professional growth, but this has been adapted for self-awareness.

Here are some questions for you to reflect on each step:

Strengths

- What skills and talents come naturally to you?
- What have been some of your greatest accomplishments?
- What sets you apart from others?

Weaknesses

- What areas in life do you struggle with (don't just focus on attachment)?
- What negative feedback have you received recently?
- What activities or tasks do you find difficult?

Opportunities

- What trends could open new opportunities for you?
- Who could help you achieve these opportunities?

- How could you develop new skills?

Threats

- What external factors could be a challenge for your personal growth?

- What is stopping you from achieving your goals?

- From the answers above, what threats are within your control?

The SWOT analysis is for you to understand more about your strengths and weaknesses. It's not designed to create an action plan. Remember that for now, we are still on the first step toward change, which is awareness.

Understand the impact you have on others

With anxious attachment, you may have found that reading this point takes you straight to the negative; you are clinging, you see problems where there aren't any, and your fears and anxiety often get the better of you. You may not take time to consider the positive impact you have on people. Hopefully, after reading the previous chapter, you are now able to see all the amazing qualities you have as a partner, friend, and employee.

At the end of each day, take a moment to journal about how you made a difference in someone else's life. It doesn't have to be huge things or even things that take up a lot of your time, and it could be giving someone a genuine compliment or a warm hug when you can tell someone is down.

Get feedback

Within self-awareness, some people will have blind spots. These are emotions, attitudes, or beliefs that impact your thoughts and actions, but you aren't aware of them, limiting your personal growth. The solution to these blind spots is feedback, which serves two purposes. First, we can see what you are doing well, and this encourages more of the same positive habits. Second, feedback helps to highlight the consequences of actions and decisions, and it even provides guidance to prevent us from making the same mistakes again.

Choose a few people from different areas of your life, making sure they are individuals whose opinions you value. Let them know why you are seeking feedback so that they have some context. You don't need to tell them your entire life history, and it can be as simple as letting them know you are aiming to improve your self-awareness. To keep things simple, use the Keep, Stop, Start model with these three questions:

- What's the one thing I should **keep** doing?
- What's the one thing I should **stop** doing?
- What's the one thing I should **start** doing?

While seeking advice, ask people from different areas of your life for their input, but stick to asking each person one thing to avoid overwhelming responses. Once they have given you the answers, reflect on what they said, and don't just focus on the negative parts.

Journal daily

There is some neuroscience behind journaling for self-awareness. The brain contains billions of neurons, with a particular type called mirror neurons. These neurons fire when someone carries out a specific motor act and when they see another person carrying out the same act. They are essential for empathy and understanding emotions and are activated when journaling.

In terms of self-awareness, mirror neurons allow you to see your experiences from the point of view of others who "mirrored" your actions. You will find some more journal prompts at the end of this chapter to help with this process.

Be curious

Mirror neurons are also necessary for learning, as is curiosity. People who are more curious don't just ask more questions; they tend to go about finding the answers for themselves, too. When we are able to learn more, we increase our perspectives, which helps us to see ourselves in different contexts.

Curious people embrace many viewpoints, and curiosity can also reduce stereotypes and biases. Build up your curiosity by exploring different cultures and religions, even if you aren't religious. Read books or watch movies you wouldn't normally watch and try to talk with people from different walks of life.

Create a life timeline

On a piece of paper, draw a line across the page and mark the beginning of the line with when you were born. On the timeline, write the significant events that have shaped you into the person you are today. This could be special events or people you met, both the good and the bad. With your journal, reflect on each of these life moments, the lessons you learned, your insights, and the personal growth that occurred.

Write a forgiveness letter

A self-forgiveness letter is an opportunity to confront past mistakes and release any feelings of guilt or shame you have been holding onto. The process of working through these actions enables you to connect with the emotions associated with them, emotions that have often been buried for a long time. If you are struggling with how to start, you can use the following line to help:

"I forgive you for those times when you weren't the person you were trying to be…"

Practice self-acceptance

This one isn't easy because accepting that we are flawed individuals can be hard. However, both the good and the not-so-good make you who you are and your unique self.

To do this, you need to see yourself as separate from your actions and qualities because they are not what defines you.

Self-acceptance doesn't mean there isn't room for change. It's one thing to accept your anxious attachment, and it's another not to want to make improvements toward personal growth. Self-acceptance is about accepting who you are in this moment, recognizing the things that you can't change, and committing to those that you can.

Practice mindfulness and meditation

Both mindfulness and meditation can increase emotional awareness by spending more time in the present, but they aren't the same. Meditation is a practice where you pay attention to your thoughts without judgment. It's a type of mindfulness, which is more of a state of being than a practice.

Being here and now makes you more aware of thoughts and feelings without reacting to them. I'm not going too much into mindfulness and meditation here because Step Five will further explore the benefits and go over some simple activities.

Take healthy risks

As we saw with vulnerability, you need to get good at stepping out of your comfort zone to let your guard down and let others in. Taking healthy risks is a way for you to step into the real world and place yourself in new situations that will offer alternative perspectives for reflection without triggering anxiety. Healthy risks could include taking up a new hobby, joining a club, or volunteering.

An even smaller step with great results would be to switch to open-ended questions. If you ask a question like "Did you enjoy your holiday?" you will get a yes/no answer. However, a slight change in the question structure can encourage others to open up, such as "What did you enjoy most about your holiday?"

WHAT YOU BELIEVE IN

Beliefs come in all shapes and sizes. You can choose to believe in a religion, the good in people, or the evil in people. You can believe that everyone has the right to own a gun or that politicians only try to do their best. Our beliefs are shaped by life experiences, the environment, and our knowledge, and everyone has the right to express their individual beliefs.

Nevertheless, there is a type of belief that will be holding you back—your limiting beliefs.

Limiting beliefs are thoughts you take to be absolute truths, whether they are about yourself or the world around you. They are thoughts like "couldn't" and "shouldn't" that prevent you from taking opportunities or stories you tell yourself that keep you within the boundaries of your comfort zone.

These thoughts are often subconscious or a form of psychological coping strategy. It could be your mind's way of protecting you from potential pain and difficult emotions. For example, it's easier to tell yourself you can't do something than face the humiliation of failure.

Beliefs start to develop way before we are aware of them. We listen to what our parents have to say about their beliefs, and we start to adopt them as our own. This can be anything from hobbies to career choices and opinions of other people. One of the most powerful images I have seen recently was a black child and a white child holding hands with the caption, "Nobody is born racist." In no way am I assuming your parents are racist because it's just as likely that you were raised in a family that believed in inclusion and equality. Regardless of your parents' beliefs, they may have inherited some beliefs from their own parents.

As people age, their own life experiences shape their beliefs. You may have grown up in a meat-loving family, but as an adult, you watch a documentary on how meat is processed and decide to become a vegetarian. Perhaps you are against divorce until a toxic partner destroys your relationship and your life.

Naturally, information plays a key role in our beliefs. Have you ever noticed how you are more inclined to believe people who you respect and admire? Whether it's a boss, an old teacher, or a politician, reflect on how your beliefs have been shaped based on those people you hold in higher regard. At the same time, these people may knowingly add to your limiting beliefs. They may have discouraged you from doing something to protect you, but you actually had the skills to achieve that goal.

Watch out for any sentences that start in the following way:

- I can't...
- I can't because...
- I'm too old...
- I need to do X before I can...
- I'm not good enough...
- It's not realistic to...
- Everyone else is...
- I don't deserve...
- I don't have time to...
- People will think...

Furthermore, you should also pay attention to the following limiting beliefs that often arise with anxious attachment.

- I am not enough on my own.
- People always leave or betray me in the end.
- They don't really love me; they're just saying that.

- If they knew the real me, they wouldn't care for me.
- If we're not always close, we're drifting apart.
- Silence or space means they're losing interest.
- Their approval is necessary for my happiness.
- Any small change could mean the relationship is in trouble.
- I must do everything to keep them from leaving.
- Being independent will push them away.
- My feelings aren't as important as keeping the peace.
- I should always put their needs before mine.

This self-awareness regarding your limiting beliefs is the first step to changing them.

CHANGE YOUR BELIEFS, CHANGE YOUR LIFE

Regardless of what you believe in at this point, your beliefs aren't static and can be changed. The body takes information from the environment and sends messages to the brain through our senses. Inside the brain, these sensory messages are filtered as they move through synapses and make their way to an area of higher processing.

It's our beliefs that determine what information makes it through to the higher processing area. By changing your thoughts, you can receive different sensory information that opens your mind to new opportunities (Rao et al., 2009).

It's not just that your beliefs can hold you back. When your beliefs can influence the way you interpret events, your feelings, and your actions, there is a risk of self-fulfilling prophecies. This is a belief that something will happen, causing your actions to make the expected outcome happen.

Let's say you are expecting your relationship to go wrong, so you start putting less effort into it. However, all relationships require effort, and without yours, the relationship inevitably ends.

Consider if any of these limiting beliefs and possible behaviors relate to your life:

- You feel powerless, so you stop standing up for yourself.

- You don't feel your opinions are worth hearing, so you don't speak up for yourself.

- You feel that everything needs to be perfect, so you get stuck procrastinating.

- You feel worthless, so you become defensive.

- You don't believe you can handle conflict, so you give in to others.

These are just a handful of examples, and while you may relate to them, it's necessary that you accurately identify your self-limiting beliefs in order to change your thought patterns. Begin by writing down any negative thoughts you have that prevent personal growth.

Then, work your way through the following six questions:

- Why do you believe this?

- When did you start believing this?

- Where did this belief come from? Was it something you have told yourself or something others have told you?

- Who in your life has the same belief?

- What specifically happened for you to believe this? What could happen if you could change this belief?

- How does this belief make you feel? How does it impact your life?

The questions require deep reflection so that you can understand the extent of how your limiting beliefs have affected your life.

However, you can't just focus on the moments when you thought these beliefs were true. If your belief is that you don't know how to handle conflict and you only reflect on the times when conflicts didn't go well, you are going to reaffirm your belief. Also, think back on times when your thoughts didn't turn out to be true.

This deep reflection gives you the chance to look for the evidence supporting and contrasting your limiting thoughts, which is the cornerstone of challenging any type of negative thought. Once you can find this balance that reflects your emotions and behaviors, you have the foundations for creating a new belief and, therefore, new behaviors.

If we stick to the same belief of not being able to handle conflict, there are several ways we can rephrase this belief so that it serves a better purpose.

You can highlight your areas of improvement but recognize what you do well—"I'm not good at completely managing my emotions yet, but I can express my needs," Notice the use of the word "yet," and by adding this word, you are stating that there is room for improvement.

Alternatively, you can phrase this as a comparison between you in the past and the future. "In the past, I couldn't handle conflicts, but I'm working on it, and I am improving." Or you can choose a more affirming statement such as "I am good at handling conflict."

Once you have reframed the thoughts surrounding your limiting belief, it's time to develop good habits, actions, and behaviors to reinforce the new belief.

If you used to think that you were not enough on your own, now is the time to start stepping out of your comfort zone and doing more things by yourself, even if that means just starting with a walk around the block alone. If you are now telling yourself that you are going to prioritize your needs so that you have what it takes to achieve your goals, it's essential that you make time for yourself.

Even then, it's not to say that your limiting beliefs won't come back every now and again. When this does, don't be too hard on yourself. But you should have the power to stop the thought in the moment before it escalates. Remind yourself of the evidence against this thought and the recent progress you have made to further support your new belief.

MAKE SURE YOUR BELIEFS ARE ALIGNED WITH YOUR VALUES

Finding your way in life and making big decisions takes a clear understanding of your beliefs, but your beliefs have to match your values. Your values help determine the why behind your behavior and actions. This is a psychological phenomenon known as cognitive dissonance. Let's imagine you have developed the belief that you are worthy of respect, which is a core value for you, but then you don't act in a way that requires people to respect you. This can lead to discomfort because of internal battle, and you may even find yourself avoiding this misalignment.

Values are naturally different for every person. Some people will value family, friendships, or their careers above things like forgiveness or humor. Others find enjoyment, creativity, or spirituality over finances, fame, or beauty. Work through the following questions to better understand your core values:

- Who do you admire and why?

- How do you define the values of these people?

- What inspires you to take action?

- What situations are you willing to take risks?

- Who can you be your authentic self with?

- When you are your authentic self, what do you like to do that reflects the values you admire in others?

- How can you incorporate these values into your daily life?

For a little more inspiration, consider the ways in which these values can help you toward your personal development:

- **Well-being:** When you believe your physical and mental needs should be a priority, you are more likely to get the right amount of exercise, eat a balanced diet, and practice other healthy habits.

- **Freedom:** You have the right to be free and act independently, but you also have the right to self-expression and free-thinking, allowing you to open up to others.

- **Empowerment:** This value is essential for believing in yourself, finding your inner strength, and confidently making choices. It's what motivates you to take risks and step outside your comfort zone.

- **Honesty:** Being honest about your flaws and your strengths will help you show your vulnerable side and create genuine connections.

As we reach the end of this chapter, it is clear that looking inward and reflecting on who you are as an individual isn't just the first step to overcoming your anxious attachment. It's about getting to know the real you and the direction that you want to take in life. That's not to say that we go to the other extreme of anxious attachment and develop an attitude where it's all about you and that you don't need others in your life.

The point of self-awareness is to see yourself as a whole and capable person, accepting the good and the not-so-good and then aligning your beliefs and values so that your actions and behaviors can take you toward the person you want to be. Your worth isn't defined by the people in your life or the relationships you have, and the relationships you have can't be there to "complete you."

As promised, here are some journal prompts that will continue to help you boost your self-awareness:

- How would you describe yourself to a stranger?

- What are the three most important things in your life right now?

- Describe a fantastic day you had recently.

- What is one situation that you could have handled better recently?

- Do your behaviors come from impulses, emotions, or a thought process?

- Does your job align with your values and beliefs?

- What dreams did you have as a teenager that you have left behind?

- What are the positive aspects of your health right now? What needs to change?

- What is one thing that you would regret in the future if you don't do it now?

- Who brings out your best qualities?

- If you could go back to school, what would you want to learn?

- When was the last time life pleasantly surprised you?

When using these journal prompts, along with others in the book, try to make it a regular practice. Many people's beliefs and values can change over time. Maintaining self-awareness will allow them to recognize and effectively respond to these changes.

With this newfound understanding of who you are, you will be in a better and mentally safer position to start working on the anxious thoughts that are affecting your relationships and overall well-being!

STEP FIVE: SOOTHING THE MIND

Peace comes from within. Do not seek it without.

SIDDHĀRTHA GAUTAMA

Some years ago, I found myself chasing something, but I couldn't put my finger on what it was. It wasn't anything tangible, and I didn't want more of anything. In fact, it was quite the opposite.

I was chasing the idea of less—less stress, less rushing, less mental chatter. Each morning, I would tell myself that this was going to be the day I found my much-needed peace. But it never came.

As the great Buddha said, the peace we all seek doesn't come from the external aspects of our lives. Having 30 minutes of free time is great, but if you can't quiet your mind, you won't find peace.

In the previous chapter, we discussed how we can change the thoughts that arise from our limiting beliefs. However, this might not be enough when a single thought spirals into a pattern of overthinking.

TANGLES OF THOUGHTS

Our brains have the amazing ability to produce complex thoughts that allow us to make decisions, solve problems, process information, and connect within society. There is no doubt that thinking is crucial and generally useful. The billions of neurons in the brain that create trillions of synapses work at lightning speed to create our thoughts. With a speed of 300 miles per hour, your brain produces approximately 70,000 thoughts each day (Cleveland Clinic, n.d.).

While this might sound exhausting, many of these are trivial thoughts. Make a cup of coffee or shower first? What do I wear? Do I have my keys?

These types of thoughts don't necessarily require a lot of brain power. However, the problem arises when thinking becomes overthinking, the act of thinking about something, often repetitively, that doesn't lead to achieving anything or isn't helpful for us.

Different studies have produced different numbers, but it's generally believed that around 90 percent of all our thoughts are repetitive, and around 80 percent of our thoughts are negative. That is what makes overthinking so exhausting. It's easy to fall into "analysis paralysis," where continuous thinking leads you to almost being frozen with a particular thought or problem.

There are two types of overthinking. Rumination involves being caught up in thoughts about the past and the present. It's when the mind won't let go of regrets, resentments, mistakes made, and situations that cause you to feel shame or embarrassment. When you overthink the present, your brain won't stop overanalyzing your circumstances and relationships.

The type of overthinking that involves the future is categorized as worry. Short-term worry could be about an event your partner has coming up, or something you need to do that is causing you anxiety, whereas long-term worry could be about the future of your relationship or whether you will ever be able to experience true happiness with this person.

For the anxious attachment type, you don't just fear the end of your relationship or being abandoned, but you also obsessively replay this thought. It causes you to overanalyze every conversation and action between you and your partner. Something that would normally have a straightforward answer becomes incredibly complicated. You may have experienced overthinking something to the extent that you lose touch with what really happened.

This is something that your partner or other significant people in your life won't be able to fully understand.

At some point, everyone will have doubts about their relationship, but many can appreciate that they don't see things clearly or that they are magnifying a problem. As they aren't overthinkers, they can't imagine having that one thought play over and over again in their minds, even hundreds and thousands of times in a single day.

Needless to say, overthinking only fuels the already challenging cycle of negativity in a relationship. Although Sammy loves her husband and her children, she has a high-powered career and is the type of person who needs time alone. Jacob, her husband, doesn't see this as downtime. He sees it as an excuse not to be around him, and this frustrates Sammy, causing miscommunication and more arguments, which only fuels Jacob's insecurities. With Jacob's overthinking, he can't break free from his thought patterns, so the relationship becomes stuck in this cycle.

Tick the following that apply to you:

- I can't stop worrying about things that are out of my control.

- I struggle to relax.

- I have trouble falling asleep because of overthinking.

- I wake up at night and start thinking.

- I tend to think of the worst-case scenario.

- I second-guess my decisions.

- I replay conversations and situations in my mind.
- I relive embarrassing moments.
- I ask myself "what if" a lot.
- When I rethink conversations, I often think about what I wish I had said or done.
- I look for a hidden meaning in everything.
- If someone says or does something I don't like, I dwell on it.
- I fixate on mistakes I have made.
- I miss out on a lot of present moments.

Before moving on, take another moment to consider when any of these thought patterns have been helpful.

OVERTHINKING ISN'T JUST IN THE MIND

We have seen the effects of stress on the body, and overthinking can lead to many of the same issues, especially when it comes to your heart health.

Overthinking may increase blood pressure and cholesterol levels as well as the added risk of unhealthy habits like overeating, drinking excessively, and smoking, all of which increase the risk of heart disease, strokes, or a heart attack.

Cortisol released with overthinking and stress can weaken the immune system. It's not just about the constant coughs, colds, and flu cases. A weak immune system can lead to more allergies, infections, and diseases.

The brain doesn't just limit our overthinking during the day. If you have a habit of waking up at night and you can't turn your thoughts off, you will feel tired, irritable, and less productive the next day. This will affect your ability to work and make it harder to find the energy to exercise. Combined with the previous unhealthy habit, you may find yourself gaining weight, which won't help your insecurities in a relationship.

Overthinking can have negative effects on the digestive system. Some people may struggle with a suppressed appetite, and the body won't receive the necessary nutrients for the organs and systems to carry out their functions. Additionally, overthinking reduces the blood flow to the stomach, which reduces oxygen. The stress on the digestive system may lead to inflammatory bowel disease (IBD) or irritable bowel syndrome (IBS) (Gupta, 2022).

As if your physical health wasn't enough, overthinking can have severe consequences on your mental health. It's a bit of a chicken-and-egg conundrum. Stress and anxiety lead to overthinking, but at the same time, overthinking can increase stress and anxiety. Overthinking isn't a recognized mental disorder, but it has been linked to mental health conditions, including depression, anxiety disorders, obsessive-compulsive disorder, and post-traumatic stress disorder (Witmer, 2023).

It goes without saying that someone with an anxious attachment is going to overthink every aspect of a relationship. We have discussed being suspicious from your point of view, but have you ever considered how your doubts make them feel? Each time you accuse them of doing something they aren't guilty of, you are questioning their character and morals. There is only so much a person can take of this, especially if they are always trying to do their best.

The reality is that your overthinking has caused you to become paranoid. It's not fair to assume that anxious attachment only causes fear of infidelity. This paranoia can extend to illness, accidents, natural disasters, or any event that could result in you being alone. Depending on your partner, they may end up changing and not doing the things they love in an effort to keep you calm, but because this doesn't happen, they start begrudging the changes they made.

If you consistently try to see things from their point of view, it's hard to handle anxious attachment when emotions are all over the place, and your partner isn't sure which extreme to expect from you.

Because overthinking isn't solving any problems, you won't be making any progress in your relationship. It's more probable that your overthinking leads to more problems. You are unintentionally stuck in a trap of only seeing problems, causing your partner to feel overwhelmed by problems that most likely don't even exist. That's not to say that the problems aren't real for you.

Remember the analogy of the papercuts? Overthinking is the same! Each time you overthink is another papercut that adds to your relationship anxiety, slowly killing the relationship. It sucks out all the happiness that you both could have, and the worst part is the self-fulfilling prophecy — the other person reaches a point where they can't handle it anymore, and they start looking for ways to end the relationship.

It's not all bad. Acknowledging your overthinking and understanding it better means you can take the next steps to ensure you aren't left alone overanalyzing how your overthinking ended a relationship. Before we find out how to prevent this, we need to clarify the difference between productive and unproductive thought patterns.

IS YOUR OVERTHINKING PRODUCTIVE?

We have just dedicated an entire chapter to self-awareness, which requires an awful lot of thinking. So, isn't this just another case of overthinking? The difference between overthinking and self-reflection is that self-reflection is productive. What you think about makes way for learning and personal growth.

It's not the time or energy you spend with your thoughts that determines overthinking. You could spend 10 minutes thinking about something or 10 hours; the point will always be whether that time you spend has led to a positive outcome—has it solved a problem?

One of my daily frustrations is deciding what to make for dinner, and it's often something I can start thinking about straight after lunch!

First, I have to consider the meals the kids have had in school so that it's something different, and of course, it should differ from the dinner we had the previous night. I also need to think about fussy eaters and how everyone is going to want something that they like, and then, with any luck, I can find some ingredients that will tick all the boxes.

The dinner thought may pop into my head once an hour and last 5 minutes. Overthinking would mean that each time I consider what to make for dinner, I get stuck questioning why my family can't just be less fussy and eat what's in front of them or wishing I had bought chicken instead of fish. Nothing is constructive or helps me solve the problem.

On the other hand, if each time the dinner thought pops into my head and I can work through one of my mini problems to help answer the original question, I know I am making productive use of my thinking time.

In the context of anxious relationships, overthinking prevents you from constructive problem-solving. What do you achieve when you constantly tell yourself that you will end up growing old alone? What could you achieve when you put this time toward overcoming your anxious attachment?

The following question is potentially quite frightening, but it's a real eye-opener. Think about how many hours you spent overthinking last week. Let's lowball it and say an hour a day. That's 7 hours that you have not only lost but also given time and energy away while adding to your stress and anxiety. It's more likely that your overthinking occupied a couple of hours daily. That's over 700 hours a year that could be put to much better use.

Next time you find yourself caught in your mind, ask yourself the following questions to understand if you are solving a problem or overthinking:

• Is there a solution to this problem? If there is no solution or it's out of your control, you might be stuck in wishful thinking.

• Are you focusing on the problem or actively looking for a solution? The solution to anxious attachment isn't going to come from your partner; it has to come from you. Focusing on your partner is focusing on the problem (how you view their emotions and behaviors), not the solution (how you are going to handle your anxiety).

• What is this thought accomplishing? If you are thinking about a conversation you had with your partner, are you replaying the same words and emotions, or has this given you a chance to see things from their perspective and learn something?

If you find that your thinking is leading you to answers and solutions, that's great! If not, it's time to move on to calming the stormy mind!

FINDING CALM

You might be thinking at this point that I am a little obsessed with this papercut analogy, but it opened my eyes and mind to so much. The first papercut hurts, but while you are focusing on the pain of the first cut, it's easy to miss the second cut. Thoughts are so similar.

You may notice that first thought, but as you are so focused, you don't recognize that the original thought has spiraled into overthinking. In order to stop overthinking, you have to recognize that you are caught in the trap.

Step 1: Identifying Overthinking

The mind is so busy, so it's not just a case of stopping the brain once you find yourself caught in the same thought patterns. From personal experience, it's best to focus on the physical reaction your body has when you start overthinking. How is the tension in your body? Can you feel that weight putting pressure on you? Are you blindsided by the sudden need to get more oxygen?

I am blessed to be able to write books, not just for the connection with others but because it gave me the opportunity to spot overthinking. With one-on-one connections, it was easier to be in the moment, but alone at my computer, I would notice moments where I would blame "writer's block," but in reality, one thought distracted me, and my overthinking then took over. Pay attention to those moments when you are more distracted because these are the times when overthinking creeps in.

Those who tell you to stop overthinking are only trying to help, but we know it's not that easy. At the same time, how you stop thinking can also depend on your personality.

One technique is to visualize a stop sign. Much like driving, you can be on the road for miles, but that stop sign is an automatic warning of danger. Nevertheless, I also understand that for some, this visualization may not be enough or may even cause more overthinking. After all, what is the danger behind visualizing the stop sign?

Flicking an elastic band on your wrist also has pros and cons. Flicking an elastic band on your wrist is literally like snapping you out of your thoughts and bringing you back to reality. Essentially, it's a self-inflicted pain to break a cycle of unwanted behavior.

The rubber band is a type of aversion therapy or a distraction from the initial problem. It can't be used to replace overthinking, so as with emotions, the thoughts still need to be processed. On this note, it's not something that should provoke any form of pleasure because this could lead to self-harm. The flick of the elastic band should be strong enough to shock you, not to cause pain or even relief from other forms of pain.

Step 2: Set Yourself a Time Limit

I can't stress how important it is to allow yourself time to process your thoughts because they aren't going to just magically disappear just by flicking an elastic band. At the same time, you don't want to fall into old habits and allow your overthinking to take over your entire day. If you aren't in a position to take time when the overthinking begins, commit to addressing the thoughts as soon as you can.

Set a timer for 10 or 15 minutes, and be sure to respect this time limit. Know that you have this time dedicated solely to your thoughts.

An excellent exercise for this time is a brain dump, where you take a piece of paper and just write everything that comes to mind without pausing to think about your handwriting, grammar, or spelling. Just feel it all pour out of you.

This exercise may surprise you, and by the end of the time, your paper may contain a few thoughts that were deep down in the subconscious that you hadn't considered.

This additional information will prepare you even more for Step 3.

Step 3: Seeking Productivity

This step involves changing your perspective and challenging the original thought to find a more realistic approach. You might fear that you are going to be alone forever, and this stems from the insecurities in your relationship, but your partner hasn't left you. On the contrary, they might be stuck in their patterns of overthinking, trying to find ways to help you. And this is where your anxious attachment has an advantage.

Because of your high levels of empathy and understanding, you know exactly what it is like to overthink. With this perspective, you can now see that the problem isn't that your partner is going to leave you. Rather, it's that they need help understanding you. Fortunately, there is a solution. This is just one example, but you can see how you have turned overthinking into productive problem-solving.

Step 4: Reward Yourself

There are two reasons to reward yourself for sticking to the time limit. First, which is a big one, you have controlled your overthinking. Second, it tells the brain that overthinking is over and encourages it to move on rather than continue overthinking.

Again, I find that physically changing the environment helps. So you might want just to walk away, make a drink, read a few pages of a book, or listen to your favorite song.

Step 5: Be Productive

Next, it's time to take action. Now that the problem is clear, you will be able to work out what steps you need to take in order to solve it. Rome wasn't built in a day, so it's likely that you will need to break the solution down into smaller, manageable steps to avoid feeling overwhelmed.

In the case of helping your partner understand your fears, it's going to start with open and honest communication. You may need to break this down and first begin to work on your vulnerability. You might then want to work on your active listening skills to truly understand what they are telling you instead of letting your fears distort their message.

It's important not to let setbacks interfere with your productivity. It would be hard to find someone who has conquered overthinking on the first attempt.

You should continue to reward yourself, even for the small steps you make toward not overthinking and productively solving problems.

WHAT IS LOVING KINDNESS?

Let's go back to mindfulness before we answer this question. Mindfulness is an ancient practice steeped in Buddhist tradition, and there is now an overwhelming amount of evidence to support the benefits, both physical and mental, for people of all ages and all walks of life, from schools to prisons.

The ability to use your senses to fully engage in the present reduces stress and tension. Regular practice could aid with anxiety and depression while improving sleep and boosting the immune system. Mindfulness improves focus and concentration by enabling us to tune out distractions. This, in turn, helps us make the right decisions.

Emotionally, mindfulness can change the way we see ourselves and others. It helps to make sure our values are in line with our sense of self and gain self-esteem. At the same time, it fosters compassion for others and strengthens relationships.

Meditation is a type of mindfulness, and studies have shown that 8 weeks of meditation can physically change the brain's structure. Researchers found that individuals who participated in the Mindfulness-Based Stress Reduction course and meditated for over 22 minutes daily had notably smaller amygdalas, an area of the brain associated with stress and fear (Mesa, 2023). Another study indicates that loving-kindness meditation activates empathy and enhances emotional processing in the brain (Hutcherson et al., 2014)

While there are many ways to practice meditation, kindness-loving meditation is especially beneficial for people with an anxious attachment because it can encourage self-love, forgiveness, and self-acceptance and increase connections with others.

Before you begin a loving-kindness meditation, you need to choose a few short phrases, similar to positive affirmations, that you will repeat. Examples of traditional phrases include:

- May I be safe
- May I be happy
- May I be calm
- May I feel secure
- May I be healthy
- May I communicate well
- May I find joy

Begin in a comfortable position, sitting or standing, and you can close your eyes if you feel comfortable. Some people like to visualize a person who loves them sitting with them. Slowly, take a few deep breaths to center yourself. Feel your diaphragm expanding as your chest rises, and the opposite occurs as you exhale.

As your muscles start to relax, picture yourself as a calm and complete person. Love and accept yourself for who you are. Feel the tranquility enter with each breath as you breathe out your stress.

Next, repeat your sentences and slowly appreciate each one's words. Take your focus back to your breathing as you sit with the feelings your phrases create. If you feel the need, repeat this pattern of phrases and continue breathing until you are completely reassured.

Now, turn your phrases into messages of love for those around you. Spread your kindness and compassion as you picture a greater connection between the two of you. You may even want to share these phrases about people who have hurt you so that you can start to feel forgiveness.

Finish your meditation with one more round of phrases for yourself, and take a moment of peace to enjoy the self-love you have created.

DAILY DOSES OF PEACE: PRACTICAL MINDFULNESS EXERCISES

Rather than finishing the chapter with journal prompts, we will look at the simplest ways you can become more mindful throughout your day.

Remember that mindfulness isn't the same as meditation, which requires active practice. Mindfulness is a state of being, so you can incorporate it into practically every activity you do.

Some examples include:

• **Mindful eating:** Instead of eating for the sake of eating, slow down and pay attention to the smell, textures, and taste of each mouthful and then consciously decide to swallow your food. Don't forget to absorb yourself in your senses when you are cooking, too!

• **Mindful driving:** Your journey from A to B can often be quite automatic. Next time, focus on the different sounds you hear inside and outside the car. Notice how things like steering and changing gears feel under your hands.

- **Digital mindfulness:** Be cautious about mindlessly scrolling through social media. Set boundaries for technology boundaries, such as no screen time while eating, and remove any apps that don't make productive use of your time.

- **Mindful breaks:** Use your breaks effectively. Take time for deep breathing, step away from your desk, and do some stretches to improve your blood flow.

- **Mindful walking:** Use your senses to fully engage in your environment, whether that's a forest, a city park, or even walking down your street. Make an effort to spot things you wouldn't normally notice.

- **Mindful movement:** When you are exercising, whether it's yoga, swimming, or a workout class, pay attention to how your body feels with each movement, the muscles that are flexing, and even the feel of different equipment you are using.

- **Single-tasking:** Multitasking doesn't mean you get more done. In fact, it's often the opposite. Dedicate your mind and your senses to one task to be fully engaged in it.

- **Mindful coloring:** You rarely see a stressed-out child coloring! Experiment with different art materials like pens, crayons, and chalk, or use your fingers to paint. Many find the symmetry of mandalas to be soothing.

- **Mindful cleaning:** There is a way to make this necessary evil more enjoyable by simply slowing down and paying attention to how surfaces look different once they have been cleaned. You can also observe the difference in the smell of a room or the feel of folding laundry.

- **Mindful gardening:** If you aren't close to parks or forests, take advantage of your garden to give your senses more experience. You don't need a huge space. Even a patio with a few container pots can be enough to get your hands dirty and grow colorful, fragrant plants.

All of these mindful activities are simple and don't require you to take out any time from your day. Nevertheless, if you want to genuinely appreciate a calm mind, whether that involves dealing with overthinking or being more mindful, it's something that needs to be ongoing.

Even once you have overcome your anxious attachment, there are still going to be stressors in your life and possibly moments when fear creeps in. Continuing to practice the techniques in this chapter will help you build resilience, making life more enjoyable!

Moving forward, having a calmer mind will transform the way you communicate with your partner and other people who are affected by your anxious attachment. In the next chapter, we will see what it takes to communicate with your partner on a whole new level.

STEP SIX: SOLID RELATIONSHIPS

We are born in a relationship, we are wounded in a relationship, and we can be healed in a relationship.

HARVILLE HENDRIX

There comes a point when you are so lost in a relationship's darkness that it's impossible to see how you can come out on the other side and for this relationship to heal.

You may have thought that about your situation and your anxious attachment, but after exploring the previous steps, you can now see the light at the end of the tunnel.

In this chapter, we will discover how communication can lead to finding that same light for your relationship.

HOW YOU COMMUNICATE

The way you communicate reflects your anxious attachment. In an attempt to maintain closeness and relieve some of your anxiety, you may have noticed yourself slipping into unhealthy communication habits where you can't express how you genuinely feel.

But from your partner's point of view, each time you seek reassurance and a sense of security, you can come across as nagging and smothering them. While you might see it as just asking for confirmation that they still love you, they may feel suffocated, causing them to feel trapped in a relationship where they are only needed for your emotional well-being.

Because of cognitive distortions like catastrophizing and black-and-white thinking, you may assume that your partner won't meet your needs, which might cause you to delay or not even bother communicating them.

Due to anxiety from expressing yourself directly, you may find yourself dropping hints about your needs or assuming that others are aware of them.

Past experiences may cause you to see things differently from how they actually are, and when coupled with anxiety, you may find yourself jumping the gun. This can also lead to unfair assumptions about your partner and misunderstandings if you can't express yourself clearly.

The problem here is that unmet needs can lead to explosive outbursts, and of course, you can imagine what comes next—you start to panic, fueling your anxiety and fear of abandonment even more.

How your partner reacts may depend on their own attachment style. Those with a secure attachment will likely meet your needs, possibly even when you don't communicate them as well. The problem comes when your partner has an avoidant attachment type.

Avoidant attachment means a person is less likely to be able to read the needs of others and dismiss their thoughts and feelings. They will avoid emotional closeness and even push people away to keep their distance. Avoidant and anxious attachments are like water and oil.

You may try to communicate with this person, but it's going to be extremely hard for them to respond in the way you need them to.

That doesn't mean you shouldn't try!

BETTER COMMUNICATION FOR DEEPER EMOTIONAL INTIMACY

Emotional intimacy allows you to connect with someone on the deepest of levels. You can express all of your emotions, show your vulnerability, and feel understood and validated in a relationship. It's a two-way street. As much as you need to open up about your struggles and your reasons to celebrate, you need to let your partner do the same.

We are often stuck on the idea of physical or sexual intimacy as being crucial for relationships. While this is true, sexual intimacy and emotional intimacy are linked.

Whether it's hand-holding, cuddling, or sex, these connections can increase emotional intimacy. Physical intimacy without emotional intimacy can feel empty.

Regardless of gender, it's emotional intimacy that allows people to feel safe and receptive to sex. It's what stops us from being conscious of our bodies and even our performance.

This is what emotional intimacy looks like:

- Talking about what you want from your relationship

- You don't feel alone or unsupported

- You feel listened to without being judged

- Sharing private thoughts in meaningful conversations

- Let them know when you are distressed and why

- There is care and concern for each other and a genuine interest in one another

- Opening up about difficult experiences and past trauma

- Talking about your hopes, dreams, and deepest desires

- Asking for help when you need it
- You are present in your conversations and not distracted by other things going on

On the other hand, if you are lacking emotional intimacy, you may:

- Be afraid to share vulnerable feelings or embarrassing moments
- Feel your relationship lacks depth and feels superficial
- Not feel like you are seen or heard
- Run out of things to talk about, and/or conversations are one-sided
- Frequently feel let down in the relationship
- Feel lonely, judged, criticized, and you don't know where you stand
- Be physically together but feel disconnected
- Lead separate lives

Don't panic if you were nodding in agreement with each sign of a lack of emotional intimacy and even envious of those whose relationship has strong emotional intimacy. You can still achieve it, even if you are going through the most challenging times in your relationship.

Nevertheless, you have to be the person to step out of your comfort zone and take the steps toward developing it.

Needless to say, that vulnerability is going to be the foundation of emotional intimacy. It allows you to open yourself up, let your guard down, and put yourself in a situation where you could get emotionally hurt. Remember, this doesn't imply that you will get hurt!

Trust takes time and will develop alongside emotional intimacy as long as you are working on it. You need to be able to talk about your trust issues, whether that's past or present, but at the same time, your current partner isn't the same as in past relationships, so it's not fair to blame them for your trust issues.

A good question to ask is if your trust issues stem from a need to control. And because emotional intimacy is two-way, you need to prove yourself to be trustworthy, too, from respecting the limits of your relationship boundaries to honoring commitments. To experience the joy of emotional intimacy, you need to be able to communicate. We will break this down into two sections so that you can appreciate the balance between speaking and listening.

HOW TO GENUINELY LISTEN TO YOUR PARTNER

It's normal if you can't put your hand on your heart and say that you always completely listen to your partner or other people. It's like you can see the words coming out of their mouths, but your mind is racing with doubts and insecurities.

There are various problems with not listening. The obvious is that you aren't hearing the actual message they are trying to communicate, which will lead to misunderstandings.

Another issue is that you won't be fully engaged in conversations, and your partner may take this as a sign that you aren't interested in what they have to say. Finally, this means they won't feel respected or valued.

Here are seven techniques you can start listening to improve your active listening skills.

Stay in the present

Instead of allowing your mind to overthink and worry, you need to be able to concentrate on what the other person is saying. We saw how mindfulness involves paying attention to your senses to be present, but when it comes to active listening, it's about using your senses to focus on the other person—the first is your hearing!

Avoid all distractions, and this could be as simple as putting your phone out of reach or waiting until the children are in bed to have important conversations. Mental distractions, such as thinking of all the things you have to do the next day, should also be avoided.

Watch for nonverbal cues

The next sense to engage is sight, which you can combine with hearing. Some nonverbal cues will be physical. You may notice tense fists, worry lines around the eyes, or a slumped posture if someone is lacking confidence or feeling defeated. The speed and tone of a person's speech can indicate nerves, anxiety, or excitement. Mirroring these emotions shows you are listening.

Your body language needs to be open and nonthreatening, as this will help your partner feel safe opening up to you. Unfolding arms and uncrossing legs are signs of openness, while slightly leaning toward a speaker shows you are engaged.

Maintain eye contact

Eye contact is a sign that you are present and not distracted, but it has to be used the right way. A blank stare could give the other person the impression you are lost in your own thoughts. Too much eye contact may come across as threatening.

When listening, aim to hold eye contact for around four seconds before breaking it, and a good balance is 50 to 70 percent of the time making eye contact. For this to feel natural, it will be beneficial for you to practice finding this balance first.

Ask open-ended questions

There isn't much to listen to when you ask questions that lead to a yes or no response. There is a risk of running out of conversation or, at the very least, not exploring a conversation topic deeply enough.

Imagine the difference between "Are you happy?" and "What makes you happy in our relationship?"

Not only do open-ended questions allow you to discover more, but they also show others that you are genuinely interested in learning more about them, their thoughts, and their feelings.

Reflect their words

This involves summarizing or paraphrasing what other people have said, and one of two things can happen. If you have heard the message correctly, the speaker will feel that their words, emotions, and ideas are validated and understood.

On the other hand, if you didn't quite understand everything, reflecting gives them the chance to repeat what they have said so that you aren't left making assumptions and then take action based on those assumptions. Examples include:

- "I notice you feel suffocated when I send you too many messages."

- "I sense that you are angry because I didn't trust you."

- "Am I right in sensing your frustration?"

Have patience

Just as you need time to gather your thoughts, so do others. Silence for a few seconds doesn't have to be awkward. There is no need to rush in to fill the silence, as the other person may interpret this as a sign of your impatience. Use these pauses to your advantage, and instead of preparing what you should say before listening, take a moment to practice empathy.

Refrain from judging

You know what it's like to feel terrified of what other people are thinking when you are trying to express yourself. It's no different for them. Nobody wants to feel like they are being judged or negatively received. People need to feel like they are in a safe zone for communication, especially when they are trying to open up. Show that you aren't judging, criticizing, or blaming them by recognizing these thought patterns and replacing them by expressing your empathy.

Learning more about different people and cultures can help reduce your biases and stereotypes. Don't forget that active listening isn't just an invaluable skill for relationships. It can improve connections with friends, your children, other family members, and coworkers by strengthening existing bonds and developing new ones. So will the right communication style, which we will cover next.

USING NONVIOLENT COMMUNICATION

Nonviolent communication, or NVC, was developed by Marshall Rosenberg in the 1960s, and it was originally meant to help with the inner-city violence in Rosenberg's hometown, Detroit (Gupta, 2023). It's an invaluable communication tool that focuses on empathetic listening and expressing yourself without judgment, blame, or defensiveness.

For those with an anxious attachment, NVC can strengthen relationships by encouraging a sense of security and understanding.

It allows you to express your needs without feeling that the other person is going to reject these needs while reducing misunderstandings and potential conflict.

There are four parts to NVC. It begins with observations, which are based on facts or evidence and without judgment. For example:

- "You always ignore my messages."

- NVC: "When you didn't reply to my text earlier…"

Next comes the expression of your feelings but in a way that shows you are taking responsibility for them and not blaming the other person. This allows for empathy and a greater connection by understanding your emotions:

- "You made me feel awful."

- NVC: "I felt worried and terrified."

The third part of NVC is about communicating needs in a clear and concise way. How you express your needs has to be in a way that doesn't come across as blaming or criticizing anyone:

- "How can you not think about what I'm going through?"
- NVC: "I need to feel reassured."

Finally, you would communicate your request, which must be doable. To reduce the chances of miscommunication, be as specific as possible.

They also need to be expressed in a way that doesn't have you coming across as making unfair demands.

- "You need to text me back right away."
- NVC: "Next time, can you please send me a message about whether you are going to be away from your phone for a while?"

Let's look at a few other scenarios where NVC could help you get your feelings and needs across in a healthy way.

Scenario #1: You need emotional reassurance

You want to be able to talk about your feelings and your needs but are scared of coming across as needy or clingy. It's as if communication and verbal affirmations have been put on the back burner.

"When we don't talk about our feelings and affirm our relationship, I feel insecure because I need to feel valued and loved. Can we make some time to talk about how we are both feeling and how we appreciate each other?"

Scenario #2: Inconsistent behavior

Every now and then, your partner will cancel plans at the last minute, and this leaves you in a place of unpredictability and increased anxiety, not knowing what to expect.

"When our plans change at the last minute, I feel really unsettled because I need predictability and stability. Can we make sure any changes to plans are communicated as soon as possible?"

Scenario #3: Lack of communication

Your partner doesn't express their feelings, and you end up feeling unsure about where you stand in the relationship.

"When we don't share how we feel about each other, I feel anxious because I don't always understand your needs. This weekend, could we have a quiet date night so we can properly talk?"

Scenario #4: Feeling unimportant

Your partner seems distracted, lost in work, or spending a lot of time on their phone. You feel as if you are just another task for them to deal with and even unworthy of their attention.

"When you seem distracted when we are talking, I feel dismissed because I need to feel that I am worthy of being seen and heard in our relationship. Could we put our phones away for certain conversations?"

Regardless of the situation you want to address, stick to the formula of observation, feeling, need, and request. You may need to practice what you want to say ahead of using NVC in the beginning, but after a while, this form of communication will become second nature.

DEVELOPING EMOTIONAL HONESTY

It's most likely that you strive to be an honest person, especially in relationships, but can you say you are emotionally honest? As you may imagine, emotional honesty is about being open about your true feelings with others and with yourself. And it's not as easy as it sounds. In many ways, our fears hinder our emotional honesty.

It may go back even further than this to your childhood when you saw caregivers hiding their feelings. In some situations, expressing certain emotions, particularly those considered negative, would have led to punishment.

As a child, it's only natural that you don't know how to express anger or even sadness in a healthy way. These outbursts can cause adults to become frustrated with outbursts, which can lead to suppressing emotions and a fear of being vulnerable.

If nothing is done to correct this, the same habits may appear in adult relationships. It can be scary letting others know how we feel in case they don't validate these feelings or, even worse, you are ridiculed for them.

You may have experienced this when trying to talk about your anxieties in a relationship and your partner telling you that you are being dramatic or exaggerating. In turn, this can encourage you to start to hide your feelings.

On the other hand, your reasons for emotional dishonesty may stem from the desire to protect others. Not admitting to how you feel could be a way of avoiding confrontation or heated conflicts. You may fear that your true feelings will only make you come across as more needy or clingy.

Unfortunately, your attempts to protect a partner, or even other relationships for that matter, may backfire in two ways. Firstly, your partner will never know what you are feeling, so how can they meet your emotional or even physical needs if they don't know where they stand? Secondly, you are not being your authentic self, and without this, it's almost impossible to find true happiness in relationships.

Emotional dishonesty in any relationship will cause people to feel like they aren't heard. One or both will feel let down, disrespected, or constantly under attack, and that's without adding anxious attachment to the mix. Without knowing how each other feels, there will be misunderstandings that lead to conflict. Arguing and conflict are the causes of 55 percent of failed marriages. Though just by a fraction, this is still slightly higher than the percentage attributed to infidelity (Gillette, 2022).

Emotional honesty allows for intimacy and maybe even a level of intimacy you haven't been able to experience before. It reduces resentment as you are able to let go of the emotions that would otherwise be suppressed. Additionally, it allows you to enjoy patience and love through meaningful conversations that are no longer filled with tension.

Emotional honesty is something that can be learned, and this starts with emotional safety. If you don't feel safe in a situation, it's impossible for you to start with vulnerability and opening up about your true feelings. To gain a better understanding of safety, it's time to go back to the vagus nerve.

Dr. Stephen Porges, the father of the Polyvagal Theory (Porges, 2022), determined that the subconscious mind is constantly analyzing environments, scanning for safety and danger as a way of survival. This includes people's facial expressions, tone of voice, and body language. The mind takes in all information through the senses and sends it to the brain, from which the autonomic nervous system responds. When our safety is threatened, the fight-or-flight response takes over.

The Polyvagal Theory takes this one step further with the ventral vagal complex and the dorsal vagal complex. The ventral vagal complex is associated with rest and digestion and the body's normal calm state, whereas the dorsal vagal complex causes a freeze response.

You may now understand why, when you are feeling emotionally unsafe in a relationship, you have the tendency to shut down. Feeling safe means your defense mechanisms can be switched off, and you are free to be your authentic self.

Paying attention to nonverbal cues and practicing active listening are two things we have previously covered that will help you create emotional safety. Let's look at other ways you can achieve this.

Respect boundaries

Boundaries protect us. They let others know what we are comfortable with and what we aren't and communicate our levels of safety. Whether it's a physical boundary, like not being touched in a certain way, or an emotional boundary, like being listened to, the moment these boundaries are crossed, your feelings of safety are compromised. Emotional safety goes both ways, so it's crucial that you respect your partner's boundaries, too.

Give people the benefit of the doubt

In this case, we need to take control of the negativity bias and other cognitive distortions. Everybody tends to bring a certain amount of emotional baggage into a relationship, which can play havoc on your subconscious and motivations within a relationship. Instead of allowing the brain to make up things your partner did or didn't do, focus on looking at them from a more positive place without judgment.

Be accountable

Nothing breaks down a sense of safety faster than someone saying something and doing the opposite. Accountability highlights how actions can be more important than words. When someone doesn't trust actions, it's harder to believe words. This could even be about seemingly unimportant actions like saying you will do the dishes and actually doing them, but even these small steps show that you are dependable and committed.

Show kindness and compassion

Kindness and compassion are the cornerstones of trust. When someone opens up to you, and you respond with kindness (or vice versa), they feel that they can rely on you for support without any negative judgments. Compassion leads to empathy and a greater feeling of acceptance. Both kindness and compassion promote connectedness, reduce stress, and boost self-worth.

Be consistent

The chances are that you are well aware of the impact inconsistent behavior can have on a relationship. Modeling positive behavior and being consistent yourself can help others do the same, which can reduce stress and anxiety while creating a sense of safety by knowing what to expect.

To turn emotional safety into emotional honesty, you need to start by being honest with yourself about both your feelings and your vulnerabilities. Begin by taking time to reflect on your real emotions through awareness. Then start to see vulnerabilities as what they really are. They aren't acts but a certain response to the act. Your anxious attachment may seem like a vulnerability, but from a different perspective, you also know how it can be an asset. Other acts can be seen in the same way as long as you aren't just looking for the negative aspects.

Start slow with your emotional honesty. Begin by telling your partner something that you wouldn't normally share with others and gauge their reaction. If their response is a supportive one, you know it's safe to keep sharing. Nevertheless, if their reaction is hurtful in any way, it's important for you to let them know this. For this to be effective, remember to use nonviolent communication.

At the same time, you need to make sure that you aren't "trauma dumping" or oversharing without considering how your partner will feel about the information you share, which is another reason to take things slowly. While it is generally a positive thing to be able to share your past experiences, it has to be appropriate, not within casual conversations, and ensure they have the emotional capacity to hear about your painful past. Considering the potential depth of this pain, it's wise to wait and establish emotional honesty before going into such detail.

To encourage your partner to open up, aside from modeling the behavior you hope to see, try asking open-ended questions. Questions that start with why, what, and how to provide opportunities for others to expand on their answers and a chance to take the conversation deeper.

A final powerful reminder about emotional honesty and especially vulnerability: Vulnerability is a choice, and it is something you allow others to see. This doesn't mean you allow others to use those vulnerabilities as a weapon against you. Remember the proverb, "Fool me once, shame on you; fool me twice, shame on me." Protect yourself and your growth!

RELATIONSHIP CHECK-INS

Over time, relationship conversations lose their initial spark and depth. If you think about your typical conversations now, what comes to mind? Are they mundane topics like fixing a faucet or deciding what to have for dinner? Or maybe the worst of all, asking, "How was your day?" just for the sake of asking.

The same applies to most of our relationships. How invested are you in these conversations? And more importantly, are they strengthening your relationships?

Regular and scheduled check-ins allow you to dedicate time to learning more about each other's thoughts and emotions. It may seem clinical to schedule time, but if you don't make time for it, it won't happen. At the same time, if your scheduled time is at risk of distractions, you won't be able to get the most out of this crucial time. It's better to spend 10 quality minutes of meaningful conversations than an hour filled with phones beeping and children interrupting.

If you are looking at the important people in your life and wondering where to start, this section has the questions you can ask to check in with the people you care about most.

Check-In Questions for Partners

- Are you happy with our level of emotional intimacy?

- Is there anything I have stopped doing that you used to like?

- Do you think we spend enough time together?

- Is there anything bothering you about our relationship?

- What is your personal goal this month, and how can I help you?

- What am I doing that you appreciate?

- What is making you happy at the moment?

- What can we do to have more fun?

- How well do you think we handle conflicts, and how can we improve?

- Do you feel close to me?

- What are you looking forward to?

- Are you going through anything stressful that you want to talk about?

- What can I do to make your days easier?

- Is there anything you think we should be doing more of?

- What new experiences would you like to try together?

Check-In Questions for Family

- Do you feel like your family is supporting you?

- Do you feel like you have too much to handle?

- Do you ever feel like you need to talk to someone but don't know who?

- What are you dreading or anxious about?
- Are you getting enough sleep and exercise?
- What's your favorite way to relax?
- If you could do anything right now, what would it be?
- What has worked well in our family this week?
- What didn't work so well this week?
- What can we work on to improve our family?

Check-In Questions for Friends

- What have been your low points recently, and how are you handling them?
- What's occupying your thoughts the most?
- Is your mood better or worse than last week?
- What is one small thing that made a big difference to your day?
- How do you practice self-care?
- Have there been any significant changes in your life recently?
- What was the last thing that made you smile?
- What do you find hard to share?

- How is your work-life balance?
- How can I support you through your challenges?
- What dreams are you currently working towards?

Check-In Questions for Coworkers

- What are the three most important things on your to-do list?
- How could management help you?
- What have you accomplished recently, and how did that make you feel?
- What is making you anxious about your work?
- What would you like to see more of from your coworkers?
- What has your job taught you about yourself?
- Who do you admire most in your workplace?
- On a scale of 1 to 10, how close do you feel to being burned out, with 10 being the closest?
- What is stopping your progress?
- How do you usually feel during your commute to work?

In this chapter, we have learned that it's not necessarily about what you say but how you say it. It's about the connection on an unspoken level that creates a strong sense of safety and honesty.

When you have emotional honesty and safety, it feels like nothing can shake you and your partner, even in the midst of chaos. As we move forward, the next step will delve into confidence and explore how to transform past self-doubt into a positive self-image.

STEP SEVEN: CONFIDENCE, YOUR NEW FRIEND

To love oneself is the beginning of a lifelong romance.

OSCAR WILDE

There are quite a few misconceptions surrounding the idea of loving yourself. It can feel like you are being vain or self-centered. And while some people take this to the extreme and become self-absorbed, when self-love goes too far, you end up neglecting the needs of others. Before you can start to genuinely love yourself, you will need a healthy dose of confidence and self-esteem.

THE LINK BETWEEN SELF-ESTEEM AND ANXIOUS ATTACHMENT

Some people will use self-esteem and confidence interchangeably, but technically, they are different. Your confidence is how you view your skills and abilities. On the other hand, self-esteem is about how you view yourself as a person. It includes your feelings of competence, security, and sense of belonging. It encompasses your self-identity as well as your confidence.

Needless to say, self-esteem impacts relationships, but it also influences decision-making, motivation, emotional health, and overall well-being. Let's take a closer look at what low self-esteem can do to your relationship.

It's possible that your low self-esteem prevents you from expressing your needs, and this often comes from not wanting to feel like a burden or putting others out of their way. Instead of asking your partner to pick up something from the store, you would drive out of your way despite them being willing to do so.

Receiving feedback from partners or anyone else can be taken personally. You know what it's like to feel bad about yourself only to have someone offer you a way to improve, and you feel worse about yourself.

If your self-esteem is high, you are able to see your strengths, so the feedback is taken in a different light. On a similar note, you may find yourself going out of your way to be loved in a relationship, even if that means sacrificing who you really are.

Insecurity is already a problem with anxious attachment, but with low self-esteem, you may notice feelings of jealousy along with your insecurity. This isn't because you fear being abandoned. Jealousy is more likely to occur because you don't see your true worth and imagine your partner being attracted to someone more deserving. If you feel threatened by others, jealousy could lead to possessiveness.

Because low self-esteem is affected by confidence, a lack of confidence can cause you to doubt every decision you make, including those regarding your relationship. Decisions may be influenced by a fear of negative outcomes. Research has shown that individuals with low self-esteem are more likely to stay in unhappy relationships than those with healthy self-esteem (University of Waterloo, 2015).

Sadly, low self-esteem is a problem of epic proportions, with approximately 85 percent of Americans suffering (Shepard, 2022). However, when coupled with anxious attachment, the fear of not being loved or being replaced increases anxious behaviors and fuels the self-perpetuating cycle.

You could find yourself frustrated with your partner because they don't validate your emotions, and in return, causing them to distance themselves or reject you, which further reduces your self-esteem. Lower self-esteem perpetuates anxious behaviors, and so the cycle goes on.

STRONGER YOU, STRONGER RELATIONSHIPS

For every low, there must be a high, and high self-esteem is within your reach if you appreciate what it actually means.

Overall, having high self-esteem is about viewing yourself in a positive way. It means that you love, respect, and value yourself as a human being and believe in your abilities to learn and make positive contributions.

High self-esteem is about believing your thoughts, opinions, and feelings have worth.

As well as how you see yourself, healthy self-esteem encompasses how you relate to others and how you feel others view you. Healthy self-esteem means you appreciate your own value and worth enough not to let others mistreat you.

Contrary to the self-perpetuating cycle, a person with high esteem wouldn't tolerate a toxic relationship. The insults wouldn't have the same impact because the person has a solid and positive view of who they are. They would also be more inclined to end a toxic relationship because they know that, with time, the abusive partner's behavior could wear down their self-esteem.

Self-esteem and positive relationships go hand in hand. Just as self-esteem can create stronger relationships, positive social relationships, social support, and social acceptance, all contribute to developing self-esteem.

A meta-analysis involving 47,000 people from both genders, a wide range of countries, and ages 4 to 76 years old proves this to be true (American Psychological Association, 2019).

Your levels of self-esteem probably go back to your childhood and the relationship you had with your caregivers. Children with strong self-esteem grow up to be adolescents with more positive social relationships, and this sets them up for healthier relationships in adulthood.

Higher levels of self-esteem can give you the confidence to talk about your needs and true feelings. Seeing how worthy you are as a person can reduce doubts, insecurities, and moments of jealousy. When your partner starts to see that you trust them, it can help build their self-esteem, leading to a more balanced, fulfilling relationship.

As much as high self-esteem can benefit relationships, it can also have a positive impact on all areas of life, especially in terms of resilience and coping with stress. When faced with a challenge or an obstacle, there are two types of people. Some people end up stuck in a feeling of hopelessness, looking at their flaws and blaming themselves for being unable to solve the issue. They don't have the self-esteem to face adversity.

The other type of person will consider their existing skills and identify the ones they are missing to handle the challenge. When they have faith in themselves, they will work on the necessary skills to overcome any obstacles in their way. This is particularly true when it comes to setting goals. It won't be easy to achieve your goal, or it won't be a goal. Boosting your self-esteem allows you to see that when things don't go according to plan, it's not the end of the world, which will relieve a lot of stress.

It's important to understand the difference between high self-esteem and narcissism. It might seem that a narcissist has extremely high self-esteem. Their sense of grandiosity and self-importance shows that they value themselves, but unlike high self-esteem, they value themselves above others. A little bit of empathy might be necessary when dealing with narcissists because rather than too much self-esteem, it's more likely the opposite is true. Their behaviors often mask a very poor self-image, self-directed anger, and low self-esteem.

While it's possible to have confidence and not self-esteem, it is very difficult, and you can probably recognize that both your confidence and self-esteem need to be worked on. It's not a case of the chicken and the egg where one comes before the other. You can develop both at the same time. Nevertheless, we will start with techniques to gain confidence before we move on to self-esteem.

CONFIDENCE BOOSTERS

Take a moment to remind yourself that confidence and self-esteem take time to develop. You have probably been suffering from low confidence for years, so it's unrealistic to imagine that knowing the theory is enough to wake up the next day as a confident person. Not only does it take time, but it also takes a consistent effort.

However, the following activities aren't time-consuming and can easily be integrated into your routine.

Write a list of your strengths

It's easy to think that you aren't good at anything, but you might be confusing strengths with talent. Talents are natural gifts you have, like singing or athletics. Strengths are your talents that you have developed through knowledge and practice.

Even if you don't realize it, with more than 18 years of practice, you will have strengths.

Some strengths that often get overlooked include:

- Maturity
- Passion
- Hard-working
- Respectful
- Determination
- Humor
- Teamwork
- Patience
- Attention to detail
- Flexibility

Make a list of your strengths, but remember to keep adding to them. Keep your list somewhere accessible, and read it in the moments you doubt yourself.

Let go of perfectionism

Obviously, you want to work on your flaws and gain new strengths, but you don't want to go to the other extreme and strive for perfection. There is no such thing as a perfect person, and when you set unrealistic expectations, you are stealing the joy from your life.

Perfectionism kills confidence because instead of focusing on your progress, you are constantly focusing on not being good enough.

Look at it this way—what's more important, a perfectly presented meal or a meal that nourishes the heart and soul?

Be careful with faking it till you make it

It's common to hear "Fake it until you make it" with regard to confidence, but this can backfire. Faking anything is a form of emotion suppression, which we know isn't healthy.

Surprisingly, research has shown that suppressing your emotions and faking them not only affects you but also raises the blood pressure of those who are listening to you (Goman, 2017).

Essentially, faking your confidence is spotted by others, and it's harder to genuinely like someone who isn't being their authentic self. Instead of faking it, use visualization to picture yourself as a confident person.

Be kind to your body

Developing confidence is not about having the perfect body. Having a strict diet and overdoing it on exercise doesn't imply you will feel good in your skin. Being kind to your body is about having self-respect and making sure your physical needs are met.

It's hard to feel good about who you are and your abilities when you are constantly drained. Aim for a balanced diet, enough sleep, and the right amount and type of physical activity to achieve all your aspirations.

Do something that scares you

I'm not talking about jumping out of airplanes or anything else that causes you to freeze in panic. Like stress, a certain amount of fear can actually push you toward growth and learning.

Let's take the example of organizing a charitable event. Committing to this means you are now accountable for helping others. The fear you experience is because there is a consequence on the line, and this can lead to greater effort and better performance.

Doing things that scare you doesn't mean you have to put yourself in danger.

It can be smaller steps out of your comfort zone, like smiling at a stranger or sharing something about yourself with someone other than your partner.

Never stop learning

As confidence is based on the faith you have in your skills, adopting the mindset of continuous learning is crucial. In some cases, what you choose to learn can help your career path. Other times, it could be about personal development. Both of these are great, but they can sometimes lead to feelings of obligatory learning. In order to make learning something you love, it's important to make time for fun learning. Consider your passions and hobbies or the things you have always wanted to do but never found the time. Take advantage of online videos, TED Talks, and free courses to gain new skills.

Celebrate the wins

Did you step out of your comfort zone and try something new? Did the new recipe turn out better than you had imagined, or did the smile you offered a stranger spark a conversation? While your big goal in life is probably to overcome your anxious attachment, don't forget that this is a process, and every win along the way should be celebrated. Doing so is like drip-feeding your confidence and keeping you on the path to the bigger picture.

Don't rely on external validation

It's always nice to hear a compliment, especially when it pertains to something you have done well, but confidence lies in having faith in your own abilities. You shouldn't wait for this to be reinforced by others. Consider external validation as a bonus toward your confidence, but get good at recognizing the things you do well and take the time for some internal validation because you deserve it.

Improving Your Self-Esteem

We have covered the difference between high self-esteem and narcissism, but there is another type of self-esteem to watch out for—false self-esteem. False self-esteem is when you base your worth on surface-level aspects, and this will negatively impact your meaningful connections. Remember, your worth isn't based on paychecks, status, appearance, or possessions.

Picture a student who gets nothing but straight A's and a single mom who is struggling financially. You would assume the student has higher self-esteem. But what if their grades are only because they fear being punished by their parents? And what if the mom, though under immense stress, is happy, takes care of her children to the best of her ability, and has created a loving environment despite her problems?

Stop comparing yourself to others

We live in a world of irony! People fight for equal rights in a demonstration but then have to rush home to make dinner for their partners. Others capture the perfect couple's photo and post it online but then do not speak to their partner for the rest of the day. Since the dawn of likes and shares, people have gotten good at only letting others see what they want them to see—a far reflection of reality. For you, you scroll through social media and wonder why your life can't be more like theirs. Each person is on their own path, and comparing yourself to others is not only unproductive, but it's also causing you unnecessary harm.

In the words of Baz Luhrmann's "Everybody's Free": "Sometimes you're ahead, sometimes you're behind. The race is long, and in the end, it's only with yourself."

Take yourself on a date

Taking yourself on a date is good for self-esteem and confidence. First, you get to try new places and alone, which are small steps out of your comfort zone. Secondly, this intentional time alone gives you a chance to practice self-love and self-discovery and shows that you are committed to yourself, helping reduce the need for external validation. Instead of being influenced by others' needs and preferences, you are free to do the things you love.

Choose self-esteem affirmations

Try adding some of these affirmations to your daily practice:

- I am true to myself

- My challenges are opportunities to grow

- I am able to reach my goals

- My strength and resilience enable me to overcome obstacles

- I am in control
- I have a positive impact
- I am in control of my happiness
- I choose self-love over self-doubt
- I embrace my uniqueness
- I am loved for who I am

Talk to yourself in the third person

This is a technique used by politicians, athletes, and many other celebrities, but it's not a sign of their super-inflated egos. Talking to yourself in the third person is a form of physiological distancing. Instead of addressing yourself as "you," you would use your name.

When this happens, you reduce the brain activity linked to negative self-talk without the same effort as techniques such as cognitive reframing. In times of stress, referring to yourself by your name can allow for emotional distancing and better decision-making.

Volunteer

Volunteering can help you with your self-awareness because it's an opportunity to learn more about your purpose in life.

It can boost confidence as you can see that your actions have a positive effect on the lives of others. And, for your self-esteem, it helps solidify your identity and take pride in your accomplishments.

Overall, giving back to the community increases life satisfaction. There are so many ways to volunteer, including donating items, cleaning up areas of your local area, spending time with children and the elderly in hospitals, or even mentoring.

Journal for self-worth

To avoid the trap of false self-esteem, use the following journal prompts to help you discover your true self-worth.

- How would a close friend describe you?
- In what ways do you feel good about yourself?
- When have you shown courage recently?
- List three qualities you have that are valuable to the people in your life.
- What can you learn from your biggest success?
- How can you help others when they talk negatively about themselves?
- Who would be deeply affected if you weren't in their lives?
- List five new things you want to try and why you haven't done them yet.
- What situations make you feel powerful?

- What is your purpose in life?

Practice gratitude

Taking time to consider the good things in your life encourages reflection on things that make you feel happy, optimistic, and satisfied while reducing thoughts of negativity and envy of others. When you stop to figuratively smell the roses, you will realize there is plenty to be positive about. In turn, this can improve your self-image and increase positive thoughts about who you are as a person.

While it's natural to begin by thinking of the bigger aspects of your life, practicing gratitude is also about recognizing the smaller things to be thankful for. It goes without saying that I am grateful for my family and the roof over my head, but I'm also grateful to the person who kindly lets me merge into traffic or the aroma of freshly brewed coffee in the morning. At the end of each day, ask yourself what you can be grateful for, journal about it, and don't forget to share your messages of gratitude with others.

Get creative

Though we know the brain is more complex, for the sake of this activity, imagine your brain works in two gears: analytical and creative. When you are in analytical gear, your brain is judging. When you switch to your creative gear, you are free to express yourself without the fear of judgment. You can silence the inner critic and be your authentic self.

Creativity and self-esteem actually have a positive cycle. The more creative you become, the better you are at problem-solving because you are able to adapt the way you think, seeing things from different perspectives. The better you are at problem-solving, the faster your self-esteem will grow.

With this in mind, explore different areas of creativity, from art to music, dancing to baking. You aren't striving for perfection. Creativity is subjective, which means it's personal to you, not there to please others.

As much as self-esteem and confidence are going to benefit your relationships, it's essential that you remember that you aren't working on these parts of yourself because of your relationship. It's the other way around.

Your self-esteem and confidence will help you become a whole person, and when you are a whole person, your relationships can thrive.

Nevertheless, for complete success in a relationship, there has to be balance. In our final step, we will complete the **Feel-Good** framework, not just by working on ourselves but also by creating the essential balance between codependency and interdependence.

STEP EIGHT: ME-TIME AND WE-TIME

Let there be spaces in your togetherness,

And let the winds of the heavens dance between you.

Love one another but make not a bond of love:

Let it rather be a moving sea between the shores of your souls.

Fill each other's cup but drink not from one cup.

Give one another of your bread, but eat not from the same loaf.

Sing and dance together and be joyous, but let each one of you be alone,

Even as the strings of a lute are alone though they quiver with the same music.

Give your hearts, but not into each other's keeping.

KHALIL GIBRAN, THE PROPHET

There are a lot of beautiful references in Gibran's quote, but the one that rings the loudest for me is about filling each other's cups but not drinking from just one.

It reminds me of another expression: "You can't pour from an empty cup." Though the latter is related to self-care and making sure you are taking care of your needs to take care of all the other responsibilities, the messages of both expressions are clear. Each relationship should have two cups. While you can contribute to both, even take a sip from each other's, you can't depend on your partner's cup.

CODEPENDENCY VS INTERDEPENDENCE

Let's tackle codependency first. When you are codependent, you are dependent on someone to the extent that it negatively affects your relationship and their life. It's not just physical support like helping you when you can't complete everything you need to do. Of course, you will depend on your partner regarding things like managing the house or caring for the children.

Codependency means an overreliance on another person for motivation, self-worth, and validation.

Codependency has a habit of reinforcing negative behaviors. You may start by requiring some form of support from another person, such as validation. The partner takes on the role of the validator, which leads to you relying on them for this validation.

If this cycle continues, you may find yourself in a state of engulfment where you not only doubt who you are as a person but also begin to feel like you can't live without your partner. When engulfment becomes traumatic, it's known as enmeshment.

Research has shown that children who grow up experiencing family enmeshment often develop envious attachment styles and are likely to create enmeshed families later in life (The Attachment Project, n.d.).

On the other hand, codependency can also mean that you place the needs and wishes of others so far above your own that you neglect yourself. Essentially, this is fulfilling a different type of need of your own, the need to be loved and not abandoned, yet it's still unhealthy.

Instead of explaining the link between codependency and anxious attachment, I will list the signs of codependency. And now, with your extensive knowledge, you can see how many of these signs overlap and relate to you.

- You constantly seek approval
- Your self-worth depends on what people think about you
- You take on more than you can handle in the hope of praise
- You take on more than you can handle to ease the load of others

- You accept the blame for things that aren't your fault
- You apologize when the fault isn't yours
- You avoid conflict
- You ignore your own wishes
- You are overly worried about your partner's behaviors
- You attempt to make decisions for your partner
- You feel guilty when spending time on yourself instead of others
- You do things to make others happy, even when you don't want to
- You put your partner on a pedestal
- You fear rejection and/or abandonment

Like everything we have discussed with anxious attachment, there is a difference between the odd moment and excessiveness.

Sometimes, your partner might ask something of you, and although you are exhausted, you do it. Or they might have a long trip and are driving for hours, so you worry. These examples are not the same as the extreme that affects how you both live.

Before we cover interdependence, there is another extreme to be aware of. Hyper-independence is the attempt to be fully independent to the extent that it's not helpful.

Typically, hyper-independence is associated with avoidant attachment, but in the case of anxious attachment, you need to be aware of your attempts to become independent. This leads to the other extreme, where the need to be independent prevents you from asking for any form of help, physical or emotional.

It's not that hyper-independence is likely to be a problem for you right now, but as you aim toward the balance, you should watch out for the following signs that might suggest you are nearing the other extreme.

- You have an unhealthy relationship with overachieving

- You can't delegate when you need support or help

- You can't let your guard down and let others in, mainly because you feel it's not necessary

- You take the previous point to the extent of being secretive

- Your fear of being let down causes you to mistrust others

- The lack of vulnerability and opening up means you don't have many close relationships

When examining the list, there are a few more overlaps, making it clearer to see the intricate balance in relationships.

While avoidant and anxious attachment appear on opposite ends of the scale, it's these overlaps in dependency that highlight how the two attract each other.

They don't balance each other out. They just drain the cups.

Interdependence doesn't mean that you don't rely on each other for support. It just means that the amount of support given and received is equal, and there is no abuse of power.

Autonomy is maintained, and boundaries are respected. Problems are shared, but they don't become a burden for either party. Responsibilities are shared, and communication is open and honest. Because both people in the relationship feel secure, they can explore their individual paths and grow while evolving together as a couple.

The result of codependency is similar to anxious attachment. Apart from it being hard to see the balance between codependency and interdependence, you end up being too concerned about your partner's needs and adapting your own behavior and thoughts just to feel validated.

Your goals, interests, and identity are put on the back burner for fear of being abandoned. Your relationships are fragile because both of you could be feeling frustrated, resentment, and emotional exhaustion.

It sounds like all this exhaustion and confusion requires a lot of effort to overcome, but the majority of the problems caused by codependency can be resolved by doing one thing— setting boundaries.

DRAWING THE LINE

When you hear the word boundaries, your mind might go straight to strict limits that can't be crossed. It can feel like you are being cold when, if set correctly, the opposite is actually true. Healthy boundaries are about taking responsibility for your emotions and actions while protecting yourself and your values.

At the same time, boundaries in a relationship mean that you don't take responsibility for the other person's emotions or actions.

For example, if you tell your partner they can't go out because it makes you feel insecure, you have poor boundaries because you aren't accepting your emotions.

If your partner tells their friends they can't go out because you're jealous, it shows that both of you are not taking responsibility for your actions and are instead blaming each other for your emotions. This contributes to a vicious cycle of reinforcing codependency.

If you look at boundaries from the perspective of attachment theory, it's easy to see how poor boundaries become the norm. When you have one person who is anxious, they won't set boundaries or will break them to please their partner.

On the other hand, the avoidant partner may have incredibly rigid boundaries, especially when it comes to keeping emotional distance.

Boundaries are crucial for several reasons. They are a form of self-care, making sure you are aware of your needs and not letting others disrespect your rights to take care of those needs. Boundaries give you a chance to express what is okay and what isn't.

Instead of thinking of boundaries as walls that block others out, picture your boundaries as a layer of protection around your identity. When you have the necessary boundaries to protect your identity and not bend or change for others, your self-esteem starts to grow. Not compromising on your values and needs takes the circle back to self-care, which also boosts self-esteem. This much-needed boost in self-esteem encourages more independence, knowing you have what it takes to achieve things as an individual.

For your relationship, boundaries can reduce conflicts. Instead of dancing around where you both stand, your relationship expectations are clearly communicated. If your partner behaves in a way that fuels your anxiety, instead of letting it eat away at you until things escalate into a fight, you have the skills necessary to explain the behavior. In most cases, making them aware of your boundaries is enough. If they don't respect your boundaries, there are consequences in place.

Again, this may seem harsh, but boundaries work both ways. As much as boundaries are there to protect you, your partner also needs to set boundaries so that the same benefits apply to them. Going back to the cups, boundaries ensure that both cups are full and respected, but life isn't so rigid that you can't take a sip from each other once in a while.

Before discovering how to set healthy boundaries, you need to take some time to contemplate the areas of your relationship and your life that need stronger limits.

Boundaries aren't only going to help your romantic relationship, but they can also improve any relationship where you feel codependency and interdependence are out of balance.

- **Physical boundaries:** These are necessary to protect your personal space and your body. They determine what type of physical contact you are comfortable with, your privacy, and what is acceptable within your physical space, such as your home.

- **Sexual boundaries:** You may feel like these are more relevant for new relationships, but as time goes on, you might realize that your physical intimacy has changed. If you don't communicate these changes to your partner, it's as if you assume they should know.

- **Emotional/mental boundaries:** Having these types of boundaries allows others to know that you have the right to your thoughts and feelings and not have them criticized or as if they aren't validated. For emotional safety and honesty, you will need these boundaries.

- **Spiritual/religious boundaries:** You have the right to believe in what you want to and have those rights respected, whether that's attending a church or worshiping Mother Nature.

- **Financial/material boundaries:** It's normal that in long-term relationships, there are shared expenses and items in the home that you buy together. That being said, you both have the right to your own money and to purchase your own possessions. It's also important that joint expenses are fair.

- **Time boundaries:** In order to have time for self-care, your needs and desires, and your growth, it's vital for you to be able to say no to the things you don't want to do and have others respect your time.

- **The absolute no's:** There will be a level of flexibility for some boundaries, but there will also be some that are non-negotiable. Some examples may include physical or emotional abuse or other acts that put you in danger.

The following questions can help you to understand more about where you might need boundaries:

- What is causing you unnecessary stress at the moment?

- What types of behavior cause you discomfort?

- What do you dread each day?

- What do you look forward to each day?

- Who or what drains you of your energy?

- Who or what is the source of your energy?

- When do you feel your time isn't used as well as it could be?

Next, it's time to get your boundaries clear so that you are ready to communicate them.

Step 1: Identify your boundaries

After considering the types of boundaries and the questions above, draw a circle on a piece of paper. The perimeter of your circle is your absolute limit, and the center of your circle is where you are comfortable.

Let's use an example of your partner constantly being late. In the center of your circle, you might be comfortable with a phone call in advance. Toward the perimeter, a text message would suffice. However, outside of the circle, no communication would be something you can't tolerate, nor should you.

Step 2: Communicate your boundaries

Nonviolent communication is an excellent way to communicate your boundaries in a firm but fair way. Be sure to use "I" statements so that the message remains accountable and focused on your needs.

Also, remember to be specific so your partner isn't left unsure. In the case of your partner being late, clear communication would be, "I'm not comfortable with you being late and not letting me know in advance. I could be doing other things with my time. Please call me if you are going to be late."

Step 3: Be patient

It's normal that your partner isn't used to you enforcing boundaries, and in some cases, they may genuinely forget. In the previous example, we asked our partner to call, but also within the boundary, there is room for a text message, so if by any chance they can't call, a message is still acceptable. Unless it's your non-negotiable boundaries, try not to be too rigid.

Step 4: Understand that there might be pushback

If you have communicated your boundaries and people still insist on crossing them, you need to have consequences. Again, it might sound harsh, but without a consequence, the boundary isn't going to be effective. The consequence of not advising you when they are going to be late would be not to wait. Consequences are only effective if you follow through on what you say.

Being humans, we are programmed to be nice and to do what it takes to keep the peace. Of course, with anxious attachment, you want to be liked. This makes it incredibly difficult to say no.

When you can't say no, you risk having your boundaries broken, your time taken, and being passive. It's hard to break out of the people-pleasing habit when you keep saying yes when you should be saying no.

"No" can be a standalone sentence, but if you don't have the confidence to say it just yet, there are alternatives that still get your message across. Try using phrases like "Thanks for thinking of me, but I can't" or "I would love to, but I already have plans." If the person insists, it's time for a simple "No, thank you."

IT'S ALL ABOUT BALANCE

Society's focus is on equality and the concept of 50-50. It's about being equally responsible for finances, household chores, and raising children, as it should be. However, when the focus is on this side of balance, emotional balance is often ignored.

For balance in a relationship, it's necessary to recognize that you are not your relationship. Successful relationships work on the theory of I, you, and we, where the relationship is something that is created. While you and your partner need balance, you also need to give your relationship equal attention and effort. It doesn't require giving 50 percent of yourself.

The step to creating this balance is learning how to make sure your needs are met while maintaining self-respect for yourself and your partner. For this, you can remember the two acronyms from dialectical behavior therapy (DBT): GIVE and FAST.

- **G: Gentle.** Be kind and respectful while talking to your partner. You don't have to agree on everything, but there is no need for personal attacks, eye rolls, and smirks.

- **I: Interest.** Show a genuine interest in what they are talking about. Don't start to formulate your response before they have finished. Focus on showing them you are paying attention through your body language.

- **V: Validate.** Let your partner know their thoughts and feelings are valid. This is true emotional balance because you need to see things from their perspective, respect what they are going through, and still assert your needs. You can use sentences like "I understand where you are coming from, and it must hurt, but I feel..."

- **E: Exercise non-judgment.** Separate your partner from their actions. Maybe you would have done things differently, but a little bit of empathy goes a long way. All humans make mistakes. Maybe your partner is already beating themselves up enough without you adding things like "You should have..."

- **F: Fair.** Always play fair with yourself and your partner. The GIVE acronym can still be used with both parties' thoughts, wishes, and feelings being respected.

- **A: Apologize.** Apologize for your mistakes and for the things that you are responsible for. Make your apology heartfelt, but don't keep apologizing, as you may end up replaying your blame and guilt. You shouldn't feel the need to apologize for your opinions or for expressing your needs.

- **S:** Stick to your values. Your morals and values are a strong part of your identity, and while there are things you can compromise on or be flexible with, sacrificing these to reduce the risk of conflict means not staying true to yourself.

- **T:** Truthful. Just as you don't want to hide your true thoughts and feelings, you also don't want to exaggerate or lie about them. You won't feel good about yourself, and you are likely to find yourself in conflict because of it. (Mairanz, 2019)

For the final stage of finding that sweet spot between codependency and interdependence, it's time to strike the balance between I and we. Don't forget to encourage your partner to do the same.

TIPS FOR I:

- Follow your passions and interests. Don't feel guilty for taking time to do the things you love and to do them alone. Think about what you used to do before the relationship or explore new hobbies.

- Dedicate time to self-discovery, whether through your hobbies, journaling, or mindfulness and meditation. You can't communicate what you need if you don't know who you are.

- Spend time with your friends. Your friendships are part of who you are. Friends give you a chance to talk to someone outside the relationship and see things from different perspectives.

- Know what your personal goals are. Your individual goal will provide you with motivation, joy, and a sense of achievement. They give you reasons to celebrate as you grow as a person.

- Practice self-care for you. You and your partner may have different ideas as to what self-care looks like. It's necessary to fill your cup with things that fulfill your needs.

- Trust yourself. Things may not have gone as you had hoped in the past, and while it's natural to doubt yourself, remember how far you have come since the beginning of the book. You are going in the right direction, so know that you are the one who knows yourself the best.

TIPS FOR WE:

- Don't assume communication just happens. It needs to be scheduled, and you need to commit to ongoing communication, not just when problems arise. Don't forget nonverbal communication, which can often tell you more about how a person is feeling than words alone.

- Find common ground and interests you can share. Remember at the beginning of the relationship when you would go see a movie or try a new restaurant? It's time to find that joy and curiosity again. This is especially true if you have children. You need time alone to enjoy each other.

- Trust each other. Trust that your partner isn't up to no good, and recognize that your partner trusts you. Trust doesn't just lead to vulnerability, and it also gives you the space to spend time apart from each other and enjoy that time.

- Respect each other's privacy. This will sometimes mean giving them the benefit of the doubt. Try a new perspective, and maybe they don't want to share their phone password with you because they have confidential work details!

- Accept each other's differences. Although common ground is crucial, life would be boring if there were no differences between you. Supporting different political parties or having an alternative way of doing things doesn't mean you have to argue; it's what speaks to your individuality. When you can agree to disagree, you strengthen the "we."

- Accept imperfections, your own and theirs. There is too much pressure for people to be perfect, and there is too much pressure for a perfect relationship. Take the pressure of "we" and focus on enjoying the quality time you have together. This also means you need to stop comparing your relationship to others.

Finally, remember that you aren't going to wake up one morning to a perfectly balanced relationship. There may be moments when you feel the balance is off, and that's okay.

It takes time and patience. Above all, it takes self-reflection and clear communication to make the necessary adjustments.

RECOVERING FROM ANXIOUS ATTACHMENT: SAFEGUARDING FUTURE RELATIONSHIPS

In some cases, it doesn't matter what steps we take, and a relationship is just not meant to be. Despite working on yourself and your anxious attachment, it's highly unlikely that your partner is perfect, and if they aren't willing to put the same effort into the relationship as you, you will never find that balance.

First of all, give yourself time before jumping into a new relationship, and use this time for the strategies you have discovered here. Get to know your true self, build your confidence and self-esteem, and create a solid identity. Love and validate yourself before loving someone else. This time alone will also help you to forgive yourself for past mistakes in a relationship.

When you start a new relationship, be aware of making yourself overly available too early on. For you, more than others, it's especially important not to fall into the "honeymoon" period, when you drop friendships and interests to spend as much time as possible with your new partner. Once the honeymoon period is over, you will have extra time on your hands. This could cause feelings of insignificance, and the cycle of codependency begins.

Having your boundaries clear from the beginning can greatly assist in this matter, which is another reason to take some time for yourself before starting a new relationship. When a relationship ends, there is no doubt that you will go through a change, so it's time to reevaluate your values and your boundaries.

As time goes on, it's only natural that you will have disagreements, known as healthy conflict. When you can feel these moments approaching, take the steps to calm yourself down and choose the right time to talk to your partner—the right time for both of you. Know your emotional triggers and practice self-care instead of reacting emotionally and possibly causing an argument.

My final piece of advice for protecting yourself in future relationships is to take a closer look at Neuro-Linguistic Programming, the study of how our brains process words, use these words, and how they impact behavior and relationships. NLP can improve your communication, help you to be yourself, understand your triggers, and strengthen your connections.

Although finding this balance doesn't come overnight, there might be an event in your relationship that acts as a lightbulb moment, making you realize how much you have achieved. This connection will be unlike anything you have experienced before. It will be the final piece of the puzzle that reminds you to keep working on yourself and your relationship. Commit to each other and your individual selves. You will then reap all the rewards of a loving relationship, complete with a secure attachment.

CONCLUSION

As we reach this stage, it's paramount to remember that the **Feel-Good** framework is exactly that. It's a framework for a process, not just a change. The change will come, but it is going to take time as you work through each step. Avoid forcing it or rushing through until you are confident with the knowledge and skills you acquire along the way.

We began by unraveling the cycle of anxious thoughts and worry that comes with anxious attachment, as well as a complete dive into what anxious attachment is compared with other attachment styles.

Instead of just focusing on all the negatives and problems it can cause you, we also looked at the advantages of your attachment style. Overcoming your anxious anxiety doesn't mean you will lose your incredible loyalty, commitment, and sensitivity to other people's needs.

Even though many of your problems stem from relationships, "fixing" your relationship isn't the starting point. The first thing to work on is your self-awareness, as this is what will enable you to recognize your emotions and behaviors. Self-awareness leads to understanding the triggers of your anxious attachment, laying the foundations for changing your thought patterns, and taming the inner critic who just loves to add fuel to the fire.

Personally, I can't stress how important it is for you to be able to control and reframe negative thoughts. Overthinking, whether about the past or the future, eats away at any self-esteem you may have. And, as we have discovered, because of the negativity bias and other cognitive distortions, these thoughts aren't just unhelpful and destructive, they are also rarely reflections of the truth.

Have faith in neurology and the latest research on neuroplasticity. It is fascinating how simple practices like cognitive reframing and positive affirmations are so effective. Remember, it's not just the mental exhaustion that overthinking causes, you need to protect your physical health too. Alongside these strategies, commit to making your daily life calmer with mindfulness. Slow down, test your senses, and keep yourself grounded and in the present.

The ability to calm the mind and manage your emotions will make working on your relationship that much easier. I don't need to tell you how one small comment can turn into a full-blown argument, not because of a specific or significant problem but because emotions get in the way of effective communication. You stop listening, make assumptions, and become defensive, which only leaves you feeling more emotionally drained and detached from your partner. It's like cracks in the wall that let the weeds of anxious attachment grow through.

We saw how amazing emotional honesty and vulnerability both are. It's the connection you dreamed of having that goes beyond physical intimacy. Healthy communication allows for this deeper communication, and a positive cycle begins to replace past negative behaviors: the better your communication, the more vulnerable you find yourself becoming, only strengthening your bond.

That being said, this takes us back to the fact that overcoming anxious attachment has to be something that you continue to work on. The connection you create through emotional intimacy will fade if you don't take the time for regular check-ins, not just with your partner but with all your relationships. One thing is to talk about your day, and another is to schedule time for meaningful conversations.

As your conversations develop and you learn more about your partner's true feelings, you will start to get a clearer understanding of just how much they love and care about you, easing your insecurities and boosting your self-esteem. However, you can't rely on your partner for validation, as you don't want to depend on them to an unhealthy extent. It's now up to you to continue building your confidence and self-esteem by knowing your values, desires, and needs and making them a priority. This is what you are responsible for, just as these are the same things that your partner is responsible for in their life. When both of you work on your individual responsibilities and contribute equally to your relationship, you will discover the much-sought-after balance between codependency and interdependence.

Remember Shay, who we met in the introduction? Her anxious attachment caused her to send obsessive amounts of messages and panic when her partner didn't reply straight away. She was her own worst enemy because she knew that she was frustrating her partner, which only made her fear of abandonment worse.

In the past, her partner would cancel plans to reassure her. He would do this because he loved her and didn't want to see her suffer, but at the same time, he started to resent this. After Shay put the same steps from this book into practice, she could see things from his perspective and understand his resentment, not toward her but toward having to cancel plans that he needed for his own well-being.

Today, when her partner makes plans, she talks to him about how she feels and also the steps she is taking toward her goal of interdependence. Instead of getting frustrated, he supports her and helps her achieve these goals. Now, when he makes plans, Shay takes this free time to spend with her friends, enjoy her hobbies, and practice self-care to refill her cup. When he returns, they sit down together with mountains of new things to talk about. This is what's waiting for you.

To achieve all of this and more, you must go beyond understanding the theory and concepts. It's about applying everything you have learned and putting it into practice daily. It will take more effort in the beginning because new connections are being created in the brain. With consistent practice, all of this will become second nature, and you can thrive in your relationship and personal growth.

SUMMARY GUIDE

A SHORT MESSAGE FROM THE AUTHOR

I have one small request that won't take more than a couple of minutes.

Mental health is still very much a taboo subject, leaving many people trapped in their minds and unhealthy relationships. They don't know where to turn for support, and worse, they think the relationship they are in is all they deserve.

By sharing your opinions on Amazon, you can show others that they, too, have what it takes to break free from their anxious attachment and lead a more enriching life with their partner.

Thank you in advance, and I wish you all the best on this journey to self-discovery, happiness, and secure attachments!

Just scan the QR code on the right to leave a review.

Please **use this summary guide as a quick recap** of the key insights covered in the book. If you'd like to explore any topic in more depth, **feel free to dive back** into the individual chapters.

STEP ONE: A LOOK AT ATTACHMENT STYLES

The journey into overcoming anxious attachment began by understanding what attachment theory is and the history of its development. The characteristics of attachment were defined as well as one of the biggest breakthroughs in attachment theory with Mary Ainsworth's "strange situation" study. This led to the first three attachment styles, with Main and Solomon adding the fourth in the 1980s. We covered some initial questions to begin understanding your attachment style.

• Secure attachment comes from a healthy relationship with emotionally available caregivers. People have high self-esteem, good communication skills, and are comfortable in relationships as well as being alone.

• Avoidant attachment is linked to a strict upbringing with needs left unmet. There is a difficulty to trust, and emotions are guarded. People often feel that they don't need other people in their lives.

• Disorganized attachment can stem from abusive parents. Signs include emotional dysregulation, chronic stress and anxiety, and an increased risk of mood and personality disorders.

- Anxious attachment develops as a result of an unpredictable upbringing, low self-esteem, trust issues, and a deep fear of rejection and abandonment.

- Attachment styles aren't cut and dry. It's possible that you can relate to styles, but there will be a dominant one.

STEP TWO: THE WHY BEHIND THE WORRY

After laying the foundations of attachment theory, the second chapter went into greater detail on anxious attachment, the triggers, and the signs.

There was a look at how both nature and nurture can play a role in anxious attachment development, thanks to some science behind how the brain works.

Before covering the importance of self-awareness, we looked at the impact anxious attachment can have, and not just on relationships.

- Anxious attachment can cause a vicious cycle of neediness, a partner's frustration, insecurities about the relationship, fear of abandonment, and more neediness.

- Unpredictability in a partner's emotions, thoughts, and behaviors can be major triggers for you.

- While moms have often been the focus of anxious attachment, it's essential to recognize that as family dynamics change, a child's relationship with their father is also significant today.

- Anxious attachment has been linked to a higher risk of developing histrionic personality disorder and borderline personality disorder.

- Self-awareness is key to understanding your thoughts, emotions, and actions. It allows you to see your areas of improvement but also your strengths.

STEP THREE: FROM ANXIETY TO ASSET

After a couple of heavy chapters, the third chapter offered some light at the end of the tunnel as we saw how not all anxious attachment is bad. When you look at things from a different perspective, you can see that you have a unique set of qualities. These qualities apply to your relationships, friendships, and the workplace. Once you can overcome your anxiety, your asset of hypersensitivity will enable you to create deep connections to others' needs and empathy.

- By looking at things from another perspective, you can see that your anxious attachment means you are highly committed to relationships and don't give up as quickly as others.

- In the workplace, your hypervigilance can make you better at spotting problems and remembering threat-related information.

- Though your communication skills are lacking, you are empathetic, which is the cornerstone of emotional intelligence.

- Vulnerability isn't about allowing others to abuse your weaknesses. It's about sharing your emotions, even when there is a risk of getting hurt.

- Breaking free from anxious attachment isn't just about improving your relationships. It's about personal growth.

STEP FOUR: INWARD BOUND

We began the chapter by appreciating the benefits of self-awareness, from managing emotions to reducing conflicts and improving your decision-making skills. Above all, self-awareness helps you to see that you are a worthy human being and that you don't need a partner to complete you. Then we embraced 11 ways to become truly aware of yourself as well as the need to clarify your beliefs and values. Another key takeaway from this chapter was identifying your limiting beliefs and those phrases you tell yourself, like "You aren't good enough" or "You don't deserve certain things."

- Public self-awareness is about your awareness of how you appear to others. Private self-awareness requires introspectiveness to understand your emotions and your physical response to them. Both are necessary.

- Self-awareness helps you to take care of your physical health by noticing the symptoms of anxiety and managing them, reducing the risk of chronic conditions.

- You have the right to your own beliefs, and as you grow and change, it's natural that these beliefs change, and that's your right, too.

- Challenge your negative thoughts and limiting beliefs, and look for the evidence to support your belief or the contrary.

- Reframe your thoughts to reflect the truth. Instead of beating yourself up about potential flaws, see these as opportunities for your growth.

STEP FIVE: SOOTHING THE MIND

The brain is an astonishing organ but still not perfect. In this chapter, we discovered how the constant stream of thoughts can quickly lead to overthinking, whether that's ruminating over the past or worrying about the future. The invaluable lesson from this chapter was that while overthinking can increase the risk of mental health disorders, it can also play havoc on your immune and digestive systems.

We figured out how to decide if overthinking is productive or not. Next, explore the proven benefits of meditation and mindfulness to help calm the mind and live in the present moment.

- Your brain has trillions of connections between neurons that send messages at a speed of around 300 miles per hour, leading to around 70,000 thoughts a day.

- Of these thoughts, approximately 90 percent are repeated, and 80 percent are negative—you and your brain need a break!

- Overthinking doesn't solve problems. It just exhausts you mentally, puts a strain on your relationship, and impacts your quality of life.

- Break the cycle of overthinking with visualization, flicking a rubber band, or distracting yourself. This distance will allow you to calm your mind and take control of unhealthy thought patterns.

- Practicing loving kindness meditation enables you to transform the way you see yourself, reduce symptoms of anxiety, and even change the structure of your brain.

STEP SIX: SOLID RELATIONSHIPS

It was at this point that we turned our attention to your relationship and the significance of communication. Healthy communication, such as that used in nonviolent communication, can prevent those explosive outbursts when your needs aren't met. In this chapter, we also appreciated that although physical intimacy is important, emotional intimacy is what encourages vulnerability and emotional honesty. We ended with 45 questions that foster ongoing communication in different types of relationships.

- Pay attention to thought patterns that lead you to jump

to conclusions, especially when your past experiences influence the way you think.

- Follow the steps to nonviolent communication—observations, emotions, needs, and requests.

- Actively listen to your partner. Don't start assuming you know what they are going to say or let your mind wander. Reinforce your active listening with body language, eye contact, and reflecting on what they say.

- Your emotions are valid regardless of what others think. Although your reactions may not be justified, start small by opening up about how you feel, and build on this gradually based on your partner's response.

- Consistency with your communication is crucial. You know the damage inconsistency can do. Lead by example and make emotional intimacy and healthy communication a priority.

STEP SEVEN: CONFIDENCE, YOUR NEW FRIEND

It's understandable that your confidence is beyond shaken after so much time dealing with anxious attachment, but it's self-esteem that is more closely linked to anxious attachment. Low self-esteem can make the symptoms of anxious attachment worse, but it can also spark feelings of jealousy.

What's more, both your self-esteem and confidence can help you express your needs. In this chapter, we saw why your self-esteem and confidence are crucial and learned practical ways to build both.

- Confidence is about how you view your skills and abilities. Self-esteem refers to how you perceive yourself as a person.

- Healthy self-esteem requires you to see your worth as a human being beyond paychecks and achievements. You are worthy just for who you are as a person.

- Don't expect strong relationships if you aren't physically and mentally strong. Don't fake it because this can backfire. Use the energy you would to fake it to develop your confidence.

- Similarly, channel the energy previously used to compare yourself to others into making positive changes toward your growth. Step out of your comfort zone and keep challenging yourself.

- Strategies like positive affirmations, journaling, and gratitude have been proven to improve self-esteem. Find what works for you because there isn't a solution that will fit everyone.

STEP EIGHT: ME-TIME AND WE-TIME

We addressed some misconceptions in relationships, mainly that we have to give ourselves completely or even that we have to give ourselves equally. Every step you have taken so far is like cutting a thread that holds you in an anxiously attached relationship.

This chapter cut the final cord by recognizing that you are an individual in a relationship you created with another person.

We covered the signs of codependency and interdependence and how boundaries may initially seem harsh, but they are what will allow you to lead your own life yet still be part of an amazingly strong relationship.

• In every healthy adult relationship, there will be I, you, and we. If the three aren't separate, problems will occur.

• Codependency is an extreme reliance on someone else to have your needs met. Interdependence respects a need for each other, but it doesn't mean you can't live without your partner.

• For your own mental and physical well-being, you can't afford to keep prioritizing the needs and wishes of others, and you need time for self-care to fill your own cup.

• Before you try to set your boundaries, take time to understand what areas of your life need them. Use assertive communication to express your boundaries and have consequences in place for those who insist on crossing them.

• Use the GIVE and FAST acronyms to create the right type of balance in your relationship, not forgetting that you need to continuously work on yourself and your needs as an individual, as well as equally contributing to your relationship.

The final trick to any recipe is the salt and pepper; in this case, the salt is putting your knowledge into practice, and the pepper ensures that these are ongoing steps toward your successful relationships, growth, and happier life.

I HOPE YOU'RE ENJOYING THE BOOK SO FAR!

I have a tiny favor to ask that could make a huge difference. If you could take just 30 seconds to leave a review on Amazon, I would be incredibly grateful.

If you've got a moment to spare and some thoughts to share, I'd love to hear what you think. Even a few words would mean the world to me.

Please scan the QR code on the left to leave a review.

CONTINUE YOUR JOURNEY WITH 'THE ART OF SELF-IMPROVEMENT' SERIES BY CHASE HILL

HOW TO STOP NEGATIVE THINKING

This guide breaks down **seven easy steps to tackle everything from fleeting intrusive thoughts to deep-seated ruminations.** With practical strategies, exercises, and tools, it helps you pinpoint the roots of your negative thoughts and offers proven techniques to calm your mind.

Learn how to **shed toxic behaviors and embrace self-love** and acceptance through positive affirmations and self-talk. If you're ready for a happier, more positive outlook, this guide is your starting point.

HEALTHY BOUNDARIES

Discover the power of self-love, and learn how to **set healthy boundaries – without feeling guilty.** You don't have to compromise your individuality just to be "considerate" of others. You can set healthy boundaries, and make your friends, family and parents **respect that boundary.**

Setting up boundaries isn't about being rude: it's about acknowledging that **your well-being comes first.** You can start doing what YOU want to do.

SWITCH OFF OVERTHINKING

The modern world fans the flames with its non-stop influx of information, choices to be made, and the pressure to always be switched 'on'. It's no wonder your mind is in overdrive.

But imagine a toolkit, one that's been tested in the trenches of the busiest of minds, offering **not just quick fixes, but sustainable strategies**.

With over 30 strategies to choose from and apply, you can create your own path toward mental peace, emotional resilience, and serenity.

READY FOR MORE INSIGHTS AND INSPIRATION? SCAN THE QR CODE TO FIND MORE BOOKS BY CHASE HILL AND CONTINUE YOUR JOURNEY.

BIBLIOGRAPHY

American Psychological Association. (2019, September 26). Positive relationships boost self-esteem, and vice versa. *https://www.apa.org*. Retrieved from https://www.apa.org

Andreychik, M. R. (2017). I like that you feel my pain, but I love that you feel my joy: Empathy for a partner's negative versus positive emotions independently affect relationship quality. *Journal of Social and Personal Relationships*, 36(3), 834–854. https://doi.org/10.1177/0265407517746518

Baz Luhrmann (Ft. Lee Perry (Narrator)) – Everybody's free (To wear sunscreen). (n.d.). Retrieved from https://genius.com/Baz-luhrmann-everybodys-free-to-wear-sunscreen-lyrics

Busacker, N. (2002). Effects of parent's avoidant and anxious attachment on children. *Family Perspectives*, 4(1). Retrieved from https://scholarsarchive.byu.edu/cgi/viewcontent.cgi?article=1093&context=familyperspectives

Chen, A. (2019). *The Attachment Theory Workbook: Powerful Tools to Promote Understanding, Increase Stability, and Build Lasting Relationships*. Althea Press.

Cleveland Clinic. (n.d.). You are your brain. Retrieved from https://healthybrains.org/brain-facts/

David Richo quotes (Author of How to be an Adult in Relationships). (n.d.). Retrieved from https://www.goodreads.com/author/quotes/186080.David_Richo#:~:text=Our%20wounds%20are%20often%20the,most%20beautiful%20part%20of%20us.&text=Trust%20in%20someone%20means%20that,other%2C%20at%20least%20not%20deliberately

Gillette, H. (2022, October 25). The top 12 reasons for divorce. Retrieved from https://psychcentral.com/relationships/top-reasons-for-divorce

Goman, C. K., PhD. (2017, August 2). Don't try to "fake" confidence -- do this instead. *Forbes*. Retrieved from https://www.forbes.com

Gupta, A. (2022, April 29). Are you stuck in the vicious cycle of overthinking? It's risky, warns an expert. *Healthshots*. Retrieved from https://www.healthshots.com

Gupta, S. (2023, June 16). How nonviolent communication can change your relationship. Retrieved from https://www.verywellmind.com/nonviolent-communication-7508262

Harville Hendrix Quote: "We are born in relationship, we are wounded in relationship, and we can be healed in relationship." (n.d.). Retrieved from https://quotefancy.com/quote/1710323/Harville-Hendrix-We-are-born-in-relationship-we-are-wounded-in-relationship-and-we-can-be

Jagoo, K. (2022, August 25). A father's adult attachment style may be directly related to anxiety in children. *Verywell Mind*. Retrieved from https://www.verywellmind.com

Kumar, M. (2023, November 13). Why vulnerability is a strength. Retrieved from https://womanmagazine.co.nz/why-vulnerability-is-a-strength/

Mairanz, A. (2019, June 5). Balancing your needs with the needs of others. Retrieved from https://eymtherapy.com/blog/balancing-your-needs-with-the-needs-of-others/

Marsh, J. (2011, February 9). A little meditation goes a long way. Retrieved from https://greatergood.berkeley.edu/article/item/a_little_meditation_goes_a_long_way/

Mcleod, S. (2024, January 17). Mary Ainsworth Strange Situation Experiment. Retrieved from https://www.simplypsychology.org/mary-ainsworth.html#Strange-Situation-Procedure

Mikulincer, M., & Shaver, P. R. (2012, February). An attachment perspective on psychopathology. Retrieved from https://www.ncbi.nlm.nih.gov/pmc/articles/PMC3266769/#:~:text=Anxious%20attachment%20is%20associated%20with,with%20schizoid%20and%20avoidant%20disorders

Nasiriavanaki, Z., Barbour, T., Farabaugh, A. H., Fava, M., Holmes, A. J., Tootell, R. B., & Holt, D. J. (2021). Anxious attachment is associated with heightened responsivity of a parietofrontal cortical network that monitors peri-personal space. *NeuroImage. Clinical, 30*, 102585. https://doi.org/10.1016/j.nicl.2021.102585

Porges, S. W. (2022). Polyvagal Theory: A Science of safety. *Frontiers in Integrative Neuroscience,* 16. https://doi.org/10.3389/fnint.2022.871227

Psychology In Action. (n.d.). Are there benefits to insecure attachment? Retrieved from https://www.psychologyinaction.org/2022-4-26-are-there-benefits-to-insecure-attachment/

A quote by Alfred Tennyson. (n.d.). Retrieved from https://www.goodreads.com/quotes/425129-i-am-a-part-of-all-that-i-have-met

A quote by Gautama Buddha. (n.d.). Retrieved from https://www.goodreads.com/quotes/52519-peace-comes-from-within-do-not-seek-it-without

A quote from The Prophet. (n.d.). Retrieved from https://www.goodreads.com/quotes/33460-let-there-be-spaces-in-your-togetherness-and-let-the

Rao, T. S. S., Asha, M. R., Rao, K. S. J., & Vasudevaraju, P. (1975). The biochemistry of belief. Retrieved from https://www.ncbi.nlm.nih.gov/pmc/articles/PMC2802367/#:~:text=The%20-sources%20of%20beliefs%20include,Beliefs%20are%20a%20choice

Shepard, A. (2022, January). What causes low self-esteem & how to improve yours. Retrieved from https://sesamecare.com/blog/low-self-esteem-causes#

Siegel, D. (n.d.). Wheel of Awareness. Retrieved from https://drdansiegel.com/wheel-of-awareness/

Study Mind. (2023, April 5). Animal studies of attachment -A-Level Psychology - Study Mind. Retrieved from https://studymind.co.uk/notes/animal-studies-of-attachment/#:~:text=Imprinting%20is%20a%20process%20similar,lengths%20of%20the%20critical%20period

The Forem. (2023, October 16). Only 15% of people are truly self-aware. Here's how to change that. Retrieved from https://www.linkedin.com/pulse/only-15-people-truly-self-aware-heres-how-change-the-forem-co-hn98e/

University of Waterloo. (1975, February 26). Intimate partners with low self-esteem stay in unhappy relationships. Retrieved from https://uwaterloo.ca/news/news/intimate-partners-low-self-esteem-stay-unhappy-relationships

Whitworth, E. (2023, August 24). 33 Brené Brown Vulnerability quotes

(+ context). Retrieved from https://www.shortform.com/blog/brene-brown-vulnerability-quotes/

Witmer, S. A. (2023, March 24). What is overthinking, and how do I stop overthinking everything? *GoodRx*. Retrieved from https://www.goodrx.com

www.ingramcontent.com/pod-product-compliance
Lightning Source LLC
LaVergne TN
LVHW092008090526
838202LV00002B/55